MOSES TO DAVID
VOLUME II

THE BIBLE COMES ALIVE

A PICTORIAL JOURNEY
THROUGH THE
BOOK OF BOOKS

MOSES TO DAVID
VOLUME II

THE BIBLE COMES ALIVE

A PICTORIAL JOURNEY
THROUGH THE
BOOK OF BOOKS

Dr. Clifford Wilson
with Dr. Barbara Wilson

New Leaf Press

First printing: July 1998

ISBN: 0-89221-419-8
Library of Congress Number: 96-65171

Cover design: Left Coast Design, Inc., Portland, OR

Printed in the United States of America.

Acknowledgments

A number of colleagues and friends have contributed to the writing of this series of books. One who must be especially mentioned is Mr. Garry Stone. Garry is the education officer and staff lecturer at the Australian Institute of Archaeology. Years ago I was his supervisor for his master's degree, and it has been gratifying to see his academic progress. His professional "looking over my shoulder" has been a very real help. He has acted as archaeological consultant to this series. Garry has also been more than helpful in the production of many of the colored photographs.

I took many of the photographs, but often only as slides. Garry has carefully re-photographed these and slides of his own as colored prints, with professionally pleasing results. He has likewise reproduced other prints from the collection of the Australian Institute of Archaeology (with permission). A large number of these were brought together by myself in my years as director of that institute.

After Volume 1, many of the photographs were taken by my wife, Barbara, who has now joined me as co-author of this series. A small number of the photographs have come from other friends, including Clem Clack, Jean Gordon, and John Rogers. A few others have contributed their pictures over the years, but their names have been forgotten. We sincerely thank them all. We believe we have kept within the requirements of copyright laws with all the pictures. The original paintings by Mrs. Lisa Flentge were first produced for display at the Bible Times Center in Missouri (our Creation and Biblical Archaeology Center). We are very grateful for her willing co-operation.

A very real vote of thanks goes to my sister, Mrs. Ethel Collins. This project started out as a one-volume offering, but has grown to several. She has willingly accepted the changes, even though these have meant a very great increase in what has been required of her in typing the manuscripts. She has demonstrated patience, diligence, and efficiency in ways that have been quite remarkable. By my own observation I know that at times she has worked about 16 hours a day over several days. I thank her most sincerely in the name of our Lord.

Mrs. Kath Salomons, my secretary in Australia, brought some of the work together from Ethel's disks. Most of the laser printing and final layout are largely the work of my wife, Barbara. With her outstanding administrative ability and her spiritual insights, Barbara has been a tower of strength as the new American editions have come to birth. She is a very special person!

To all these (and others unnamed) I offer thanks in Jesus' name.

Clifford (and Barbara) Wilson

Contents

In this section we consider the background against which Moses was born, including details of the royal family into which he was adopted. We see the possibility of his being a rival to the throne, and of his flight to Midian where he became a shepherd. In that area he met with God at the burning bush, and was commissioned to return to Egypt where he would be the deliverer of his people from bondage.

A series of ten plagues demonstrated the almighty power of God, and eventually Pharaoh allowed the people to leave Egypt. The Passover was celebrated before the "Exodus." The Hebrews crossed the Sea of Reeds safely, but all the Egyptian troops — including the pharaoh — were drowned. Moses led the people effectively for 40 years, despite their murmurings and even rebellion. He established them as a nation, and gave them a wonderful code of laws.

In this section we see a remarkable number of parallels between the life of our Lord and the experiences of Moses. Moses was perhaps the greatest man to emerge from Israel, but Jesus was the greatest of all men. It is indeed true that "a greater-than-Moses is here."

Joshua had been the special "servant" of Moses and, under God, Moses anointed him as leader when he himself was about to die. Joshua was challenged by the Lord to have courage and to know that the Lord was with him. He successfully led his people in three major campaigns — in the center of the land, to the south, and then in the north. He was beset by very great problems because of the abominable religious practices of the Canaanites against whom he and his people were instructed to act in judgment on behalf of God. During Joshua's lifetime the people followed the Lord, largely because of his godly example.

The period of the Judges followed Joshua, with serious decline because of the lack of true spiritual leadership. These times are well described by sin, subjection, sorrow, and salvation.

The prophet Samuel stands out as a great beacon between the times of the Judges and the establishment of a monarchy.

Eventually Saul was appointed as Israel's first king but he failed spiritually. Then David, "the man after God's own heart," united the people so that Israel became a true nation. Jerusalem became the spiritual as well as the national capital of the people.

SECTION IV: A Greater-Than-Joshua Is Here

Once again we see very interesting comparisons and contrasts between a great man of the Old Testament and the greatest of all men, our Lord Jesus Christ. It is interesting to realize that "Joshua" is the Hebrew form of the Jewish name "Jesus." Moses added "Je" to this man's original name "Oshea" — literally meaning, "Jehovah is Saviour." Joshua was in a very real sense the saviour of his people, but our Lord Jesus Christ — our heavenly Joshua — offered himself to be the Saviour of all the world. A greater-than-Joshua is here.

SECTION V: Saul and David in the Light of History

Saul, whose name means "little," was a very big man in stature, but a very small man in spiritual capacity. He was the choice of the people as king, and God told the distressed Samuel that in fact the people had rejected God himself by this choice, and not just Samuel.

Saul presumed on the office of priest and in other ways it became clear that he was not the right man to be the anointed king of God's special people Israel. David, the shepherd boy, was anointed, to the surprise of his father and older brothers, and even of Samuel. The Scripture says that David was a man after God's own heart, and despite obvious weaknesses, there are many pointers within Scripture — especially the Psalms — which show that basically David was a truly spiritual man.

After the disastrous rule of Saul, David was able to unite the people, a condition they were ready for because of their common language, their shared blood relationship, their wilderness experiences, and other activities in which they were unitedly engaged against the people of the land. In addition, there was their special heritage as the people who had a unique understanding of the true God, Jehovah.

David was Israel's Shepherd King who gave to the world the beautiful Psalm 23 which commences with those famous words, "The Lord is my shepherd." He was also Israel's sweet Psalmist, the one who gave to the world personal psalms of worship, and he was responsible for the collation of many others — possibly he was the "most popular" songwriter of all ages! He was also the courageous Warrior King who defeated the giant Goliath of Gath, and then personally led his people with great courage against very powerful enemies. However, God did not allow him to build the temple because of his shameful dealings with Uriah the Hittite, but he did leave a united and strong nation when he handed over authority to his son Solomon.

SECTION VI: A Greater-Than-David Is Here

David was a great man, but he also demonstrated serious weaknesses. In this section we consider many ways in which David's greater Son, the Lord Jesus Christ, was indeed greater than David. Jesus himself pointed out that David looked down through the centuries and referred to his own Son as being God incarnate (Ps. 110:1).

SELECTIVE BIBLIOGRAPHY

FOREWORD

Clifford Wilson is a man of the modern Christian Renaissance in the best sense of the word — archaeologist, theologian, linguist, psychologist, educator, writer, lecturer, and world traveler. Even more importantly, he is a keen witness to the truth and power of biblical Christianity, witnessing with unusual effectiveness, both with a consistent Christian life and through a prodigious output of scholarly works of Christian evidences and exposition.

This new volume is the second in a series covering the entire Bible. This series may well be the most significant of all his many books. This series is almost unique in its twofold appeal. First, it is of great value as a contribution to Christian apologetics, documenting pictorially the historical trustworthiness of the Bible in copious detail. Second, it is a work of beauty, profusely illustrated, depicting the lands and events of the Bible more completely and incisively than anything ever published before, so far as I know.

I believe it will find an honored place in the most-used portion of the reference library of all those pastors and Bible teachers who believe and teach the Word of God in its full truth and life-changing power. But it will also be a book that everyday Christians will want to keep on their coffee tables, delightful to browse in and edifying to read wherever it is opened.

I consider it a privilege to recommend the series, heartily and without reservation, to everyone. I first heard Dr. Wilson some 20 years ago, speaking on his weekly radio program, and always ending his message with a ringing declaration of the absolute truth of the Bible: "Thy Word is Truth!" Since then, we have often met together, worked together, prayed together. He has graciously provided a number of exhibits in our ICR Museum of Creation and Earth History. In many ways, he has been both an esteemed colleague and a warm friend — tireless scholar and beloved Christian brother.

Consequently, I am glad to help introduce both Dr. Wilson and this outstanding series to what I trust will be the widest and most responsive audience he has ever served. You, my reading friend, have a delightful learning experience in store!

Henry M. Morris
President Emeritus
Institute for Creation Research

NOTE: Since Dr. Morris wrote his foreword to Volume 1, Dr. Clifford Wilson and Dr. Barbara Baddeley have married. All volumes following Volume 1 are produced jointly by Clifford and Barbara.

A Brief Survey of Volumes I and II of

THE BIBLE COMES ALIVE

IN VOLUME 1 . . .

In Volume I of *The Bible Comes Alive* we especially considered the evidences for the authenticity of the Book of Genesis, as well as a consideration of the historical data and the spiritual lessons that are within that book.

We saw that history starts at Genesis 1, with a record that is totally acceptable to intelligent, thinking human beings provided they accept the concept of "God." In contrast, the records of other people such as the Babylonians are seen as distorted corruptions of the original which is in the Bible. That criticism is true of other records which are in contrast with the revelation of true history as it is given in Genesis, chapters 1 through 11, "the seedplot of the Bible." The flood, long-living men, the settlement on the Plain of Shinar, the incident of the Tower of Babel, and Abraham's family being linked with both Ur and Haran are recognized as authentic records which are superior to some of these where distortions and corruptions are obvious.

We saw also that the stories of the Patriarchs — Abram, Isaac, Jacob, and Joseph — "breathe the atmosphere" of the times and people claimed for them. The archaeological evidence supporting these records is not direct in that none of these patriarchs is personally known in the writings so far recovered. However, the indirect evidence supporting them is overwhelming — customs, words, titles, and other background evidence is of such a nature that nobody would reject these records as authentic if it were not for the spiritual overtones and implications of so accepting them.

IN VOLUME 2 . . .

In Volume 2 we take these matters further, first by a consideration of the life and times of Moses. At first sight it might seem strange to think of a baby being born, floated openly on a river, found by a royal princess, adopted into the royal family with all the educational and other advantages that such status would ensure, then move away for 40 years becoming a humble shepherd in a relatively isolated area, then returning to score one of the world's greatest-ever victories against a mighty secular power — leading a whole assortment of slave people into a nationhood that was to dramatically affect the history of the whole world.

We see Moses as an outstanding scholar, a distinguished diplomat, a discerning law-giver, an almost incredibly wise leader, and a man whose commitment to God was possibly as great as that of any other man who ever lived — apart from the Lord Jesus Christ himself.

We consider a great deal of archaeological evidence which again shows that the records of these Scriptures continue to "breathe the atmosphere of the times." We also see that the laws of Moses were not the first ever given, but were dramatically superior to all that had gone before him. That Law bore within it "the imprint of the finger of God."

We further consider a comparison and a contrast between Moses and our Lord, and even though Moses was one of the greatest men ever to live, "a greater-than-Moses is here." On Moses' death he was succeeded by Joshua, and as we study the records we are impressed with his military leadership and his devotion to God. He led the people over the swollen Jordan River, without boats but obeying the Lord who told him, "Arise and go over this Jordan" (Josh. 1:2).

A series of three major conquests followed — in the center of the land, starting with Jericho; then to the south where Lachish and other cities fell to Joshua; and then in the north where the king of Hazor and others unsuccessfully united against these victorious Israelites.

Joshua had continual conflict with the ungodly Canaanites whose religious practices were an abomination before the Lord, and under God, he conquered them and urged his people to renounce their unholy religious alliances. While he was alive this was successful, but after his death there were evidences of declension and this was especially a problem in the days of the judges when "every man did that which was right in his own eyes." A series of subjections followed the sin of the people, then when they repented God raised up saviours ("judges") and there was deliverance until the people again fell into sin.

Samuel was the last of the judges before Saul was anointed when, the Lord said, the people had rejected God and not just Samuel. If they had waited, a more acceptable king would have been offered to them, even "David, the man after God's own heart."

The Kingdom United Under David

After serious failure, Saul was rejected and David, the shepherd boy, was anointed as king. Eventually he was made king over both Judah and Israel, and he led his people in a great series of conquests, uniting them in a way that had not been seen previously. Their common language, their blood relationship, and their recognition (even dimly) of Jehovah as the one true God, all contributed to these people becoming a nation whose influence was to have a dramatic impact on the history of the world right through to present times.

Finally, we again recognize the greatness of our Lord Jesus Christ. We present a series of comparisons and contrasts between Israel's great King David — the shepherd, the Psalmist, and the warrior — and David's greater Son, the Lord Jesus Christ who was born in David's city of Bethlehem.

In Volume 2 of this series we recognize the historical value of the records from Moses to David, we learn great spiritual lessons as the principles of God are clearly seen, and through all this we are especially reminded that a greater-than-Moses, than Joshua, and David is here.

We bring to Him our worship!

SECTION I

MOSES IN EGYPT

Raamses II ("The Great") was indeed great, as men count greatness, but Moses rejected man's greatness and identified himself with the living God.

Raamses II

This is Raamses II ("The Great") whom many scholars wrongly equate with the exodus of the Israelites from Egypt. The length of his reign (and that of preceding pharaohs) does not fit the biblical requirements.

In any case, 1 Kings 6:1 tells how long the Exodus was before Solomon's time. If the Bible statement is taken literally (as this author does) Raamses II lived about 150 years after the Exodus. As with other pharaohs, Raamses illustrates the way the pharaohs of Egypt were regarded as gods.

Memphis Near Saqqara

Despite its partial destruction over 100 years before Moses' time, Memphis would still have been a major center for northern Egypt. Bible prophecies declared it would become desolate and that has been fulfilled.

Another View of Memphis

Upper Egypt was above Memphis, with Lower Egypt in the Delta below. The plural Mizraim ("Egypts") implies the two divisions. Geographically, even now, Memphis could still be prosperous, but it is virtually deserted.

Memphis

This is the general area of Memphis in Egypt as it is now. In early times it was the capital of northern Egypt, and was in fact a great commercial center. It is believed to have been founded by the first ruler of united Egypt, the pharaoh Menes.

In Genesis 12 we read of Abraham going down into Egypt in a time of famine, and he came in contact with the pharaoh. The implication is that he was in the area of Memphis.

It is also probable that the Egyptian stories of Joseph centered from this area, as it was the capital of Egypt at that time. Thus, from Memphis Joseph would have moved up and down the land. Likewise many of the incidents with Moses, including the confrontations with the pharaoh, would probably have taken place in this area.

Memphis is known in the Old Testament. It is called Noph at Isaiah 19:13; Jeremiah 2:16, 44:1, 46:14, 19; and Ezekiel 30:13,16. It is called Memphis by the prophet Hosea (Hos. 9:6). Ezekiel predicted that the images of the city would be destroyed, and Jeremiah looked on through the centuries and saw this extensive city's total destruction. Both prophecies have been fulfilled in their entirety.

Memphis as It Is Today

Today the area of Memphis is desolate, with some evidences of its greatness in the fallen statues of Raamses and the still-standing sphinx, but not much as regards commerce and building structures. The prophets warned that God's judgment would fall on the city, and it seems that the fulfillment continues even today.

Memphis was recognized as the chief seat of learning about the time of Moses, and when we read in the Acts of the Apostles that Moses was "learned in all the wisdom of the Egyptians," it would seem that this included learning about the religious practices of Egypt. He would have known of Ptah, who was so important at Memphis, the god who was supposedly the "god of the universe." He would also have known of the sacred bull Apis. Ptah was supposed to have created all gods and men by literally thinking them into existence. Moses would have learned about Osiris who was supposedly the god of the living, the deity who controlled virtually all aspects of life beyond the grave.

In this area there was a magnificent temple dedicated to the sacred bull Apis, and when we read of the Israelites worshiping a calf in the wilderness, it is probable that this is what they were going back to as they remembered the worship by which they were surrounded in Egypt.

Raamses the Great

Raamses II ("The Great") reigned for some 66 years (1290-1224 B.C.), and was famous for his vast building programs all over Egypt. He was the ruler of both Upper and Lower Egypt. Recovered inscriptions make it very clear that he was also very boastful.

Liberal scholars often claim that Raamses the Great is the pharaoh of the Exodus, but if we accept the biblical statements at face value he is considerably later than Moses' time. The evidence points to Pharaoh Thutmose III as the pharaoh of the Exodus, with his son the co-regent Amenophis II (= Amenhotep II) absent while campaigning against the Canaanites. Thutmose died at about 80 years of age, and he is the only pharaoh who ruled long enough to fit the chronological details given at the beginning of the Book of Exodus.

Raamses II's Statue at Memphis

This is one of many statues of Raamses the Great, in this case in a small museum at Memphis, the ancient No-Ammon. The site was famous in the days of both Joseph and Moses. Today it is virtually deserted, although the famous Step Pyramid of Saqqara is only a few miles away.

How Are the Mighty Fallen!

This is another view of that fallen statue of Raamses at Memphis.

Apart from the problem of reconciling the date of the Exodus with the details given in 1 Kings 6:1, the events before, during, and after the rule of Raamses the Great do not fit the chronological pattern of the Exodus. These demand the acceptance of Thutmose III as the pharaoh of the Exodus.

It is interesting to note that x-ray photographs taken by a dental team have established that the body of the man supposed to be that of the elderly Thutmose III is actually of a man about half his advanced age, and it is a virtually dismembered body.

It is possible that the pharaoh was lost in the Red Sea, and as the priests had to embalm the one who was supposed to be the manifestation of Ra the sun god, they embalmed another body. It would be relatively easy to take the body of one of the soldiers who lost his life in the pursuit of the Israelites, and embalm him with all the usual

Here is another view of that same statue. The pharaoh was supposedly the living manifestation of Ra the sun god. How are the mighty fallen!

paraphernalia associated with the death of a pharaoh. The priests believed he was god — he must be embalmed and put in a burial chamber on the west side of the Nile. That was the side of the setting sun — and the pharaoh must be free to join the sun on its nightly journey through the underworld.

At Memphis there are two great statues of Pharaoh Raamses II — one was in a stagnant pool, and the other was in a small museum. The glory of Memphis has departed — in accordance with Old Testament prophecies.

This sphinx in its deserted glory is another reminder of the glory that has departed from Memphis. There are many reminders of the past scattered around the countryside of Egypt.

The Sphinx at Memphis

Archaeologists found considerable evidence of the magnificence that had been Memphis with granite blocks, broken obelisks, and various statues and alabaster columns along the streets. These were buried beneath some 10-20 feet of sand until they were unearthed by the excavations at the end of the 19th century.

Evidence was found of four great temples dedicated to the deities Ptah, Proteus, Isis, and Apis. They also found evidence of two palaces and a great fortress that stretched across some two acres. At the same time they found the two great Colossae of Raamses II (already referred to). Then there was this beautiful alabaster sphinx standing through the centuries, out in an open area at Memphis. It is some 26 feet long and 40 feet high, and it would weigh approximately 80 tons. Memphis was undoubtedly a city of magnificent culture and impressive structures.

A good question to ask is "Why is it not a great center today?" The answer seems simply to be that the judgment of God was pronounced through Old Testament prophets against Noph, the Egyptian city of Memphis. It is indeed true that the glory has departed.

The Step Pyramid at Saqqara

One of the most interesting aspects of Memphis is that there was a huge cemetery area nearby. It was 2 miles wide and about 60 miles long, thus obviously stretching beyond the city itself. It was crowded with the remains of about 40-50 men and women as well as animals, and even pharaohs in more elaborate settings. Some were close to the surface of the sand, while others were in properly prepared graves.

The Step Pyramid at Saqqara

The making of pyramids is believed to have stretched over about 200 years. This famous "Step Pyramid" was the first of these structures. It was an elaboration of the earlier rectangular mastabas (burial places).

The relevance of this to the Step Pyramid at Saqqara is that Saqqara was a burial place for the pharaohs. Such sites were first of all mastabas. A mastaba was a flat, rectangular structure, rather simple in outline but dignified in style. There are a number of these in the Memphis/Saqqara area.

Traditionally it was Pharaoh Zozer who established the first step pyramid about 2600 B.C. — it was actually a series of mastabas, one on top of the other. This was the beginning of the "Pyramid Age." When was it constructed? Egyptian dates have a habit of coming down, and probably it was built not long after the biblical flood.

Princess Hatshepsut, the Foster Mother of Moses?

Despite the oppression by the pharaoh, in the fullness of time God's man was born — Moses, who was reared as the son of a princess. He had been hidden by his mother when the pharaoh decreed that all male Hebrew children should be killed at birth.

So it was that Moses was taken by his mother and allowed to float gently on the Nile in a little papyrus boat, for that is what the words "ark of bulrushes" mean in this context. Little Moses in the ark was carefully watched over by his older sister Miriam.

We pause to notice an interesting fact about the killing of all Hebrew male babies. The names of two women who acted as midwives to the Hebrew slaves are given. It is not so long since it was fashionable to claim that the names of those two Hebrew midwives were fictitious. They were Shiphrah and Puah (Exod. 1:15). Both names (not the actual women) are now known from archaeological findings among northwestern Semitic women of the second millennium B.C. One dates to the 18th century B.C., while the other was known in the 14th century B.C. This indicates that there were such names in use in ancient Egypt, as the Bible claims.

Moses was seen by the pharaoh's daughter, and she rescued him and reared him as her own son. Probably that princess was Hatshepsut, who in a series of complex maneuvers assumed the role of pharaoh when Thutmose II died, even though the young prince (who eventually became Thutmose III) should have been the new pharaoh when his father died. Instead he had to wait, resentfully, until the woman pharaoh Hatshepsut died, long after he himself had reached manhood.

It is very likely that Thutmose and Moses were well-acquainted in boyhood. Moses was trained as though he were an Egyptian prince by blood (Acts 7:21-22). Thutmose, Aaron, and Moses were within about three years of each other in age, and as Moses' mother was paid to care for him

The Princess Who Became Pharaoh

This is Pharaoh Hatshepsut, almost certainly the princess who rescued Moses from the Nile. She usurped the throne from the young prince who later became Thutmose III. (She was both his stepmother and his mother-in-law!)

Hatshepsut Again — Now As Pharaoh!

Hatshepsut is now depicted with a beard. The only woman to have been a pharaoh in her own right, she usurped the throne, being accepted as pharaoh until her death. When Thutmose III took the throne, he did his best to destroy her statues.

for some time (Exod. 2:7-10), it is possible that these three played together as children.

The Bearded Lady Pharaoh

Hatshepsut was the only woman ever to reign in her own right as pharaoh in Egypt. She lived up to the role, even depicting herself as bearded, because that was the usual way of showing a pharaoh in statue form. Three of her five statues in the museum at Brooklyn, New York, show her as bearded.

The time came when Moses fled from the palace after killing an Egyptian who was oppressing Moses' Hebrew brethren. Possibly Hatshepsut saw Moses, now a highly trained mature man, as a rival for her unnatural role as pharaoh, for Thutmose was very much in the background, and in his early years he seemed to be relatively weak.

When Moses returned to Egypt Hatshepsut was dead, and (accepting the early date for the Exodus) Thutmose III was the reigning pharaoh. We have suggested that he might have been Moses' foster brother. This would explain how Moses and Aaron could have had such ready access to the pharaoh's presence. He seems to have known them personally. One pointer to that is that when they were addressed by the pharaoh, he used their personal names.

A Royal Lady Boating on the River Nile

The River Nile was supposed to be the lifeblood of the god Osiris, and of Egypt itself. It was sacred to the people, but it was also a favorite resort for pleasure — as this royal lady and her attendants demonstrate.

Life in ancient Egypt is depicted by many scenes that have been captured in tombs and on papyrus. Many of them deal especially with the River Nile. Birds supposedly alight on the barges carrying royal personages, and at other times the pharaohs are shown with their bows and arrows hunting the falcons and other birds that conveniently fly just overhead. In such scenes the pharaoh seems to have forgotten that the bird at which he is firing is sacred!

Not only the birds but the fish are also depicted vividly in some of the ancient documents, as in one picture where a servant manages to club one of the birds he has caught while it was flying immediately overhead, and another servant has skillfully put his spear through two fish at once.

One well-known picture shows Raamses the Great as a skillful archer with arrows placed exactly where he wanted in the geese that run ahead of the hound that had been trained to bring them back to its master.

The picture shown here has the protecting sun disk overhead while the attending servant girls are ready to fulfill the slightest whim of their royal mistress — even to the point of supplying whatever cosmetic care she might require. The boat itself has the protecting eye of the god Horus painted on its bow, and the sacred fish of the Nile swim casually alongside. The whole scene is idyllic.

Pharaoh Hatshepsut Enjoys the River Nile

Queen Hatchepsut travels in a boat.

This papyrus from the time of Moses indicates the fact that even the pharaoh would enjoy the recreation of boating on the Nile. As we have seen, in this case the pharaoh was the only woman ever to be pharaoh in her own right — Queen Hatshepsut.

We are not surprised to find that this Egyptian princess, Hatshepsut, followed the practices of her times and enjoyed boating on the River Nile. On this occasion her attendants are all female, including the maidservant who capably propels the boat with a single oar.

Needless to say, her royal highness would not always confine herself to a royal barge such as this. Egypt has always been renowned for its heat, and no doubt many a time her majesty would go ashore and enjoy a bath in the sacred river.

One such occasion is described beautifully in the Bible at Exodus 2:5.

And the daughter of Pharaoh came down to bathe at the river; and her maidens walked along by the riverside; and she saw the ark among the flags, and sent her handmaid to fetch it.

The Princess Finds the Baby Moses

The Bible tells how the oppression against the Hebrew slaves was greatly increased. It states that a new pharaoh arose who did not know Joseph (Exod. 1:8), and over a period of time the Hebrews became slaves to the Egyptians, and their lot was almost unbearable.

Then the pharaoh gave orders for all the newly born male babies to be killed, so that the population of these slaves would be kept at a minimum — otherwise, according to the pharaoh, they would be a threat to

A Princess Adopts a Baby

Hatshepsut is believed to be the princess who adopted Moses and gave him all the advantages of Egyptian palace life. It was a real commitment of faith when Moses "refused to be called the son of Pharaoh's daughter" (Heb. 11:24).

the Egyptians themselves. At this time the baby Moses was born, hidden for three months, then put into a little boat made of papyrus reeds, covered with pitch, and allowed to float down the River Nile.

Moses' sister Miriam watched over the proceedings, and saw the maidservant of the Egyptian princess recover her brother. She came forward and offered to find a Hebrew nurse to care for the child, and so it was that Moses' mother became the paid nurse to look after her own son.

We read at Acts 7:22 that Moses was instructed in all the wisdom of the Egyptians and that he was mighty in words and deeds. He was a child of the palace, and would have had the very great educational advantages available to Egyptian royalty at this time. He would have known at least three languages, and his education would have included a study of the foreign cuneiform records from ancient Babylonia. These would have included myths and legends which at times were distorted corruptions of the true records which had been handed down through the elders of Israel.

Our modern picture shows the princess Hatshepsut rescuing the baby Moses from the River Nile.

Thothmes III — The Foster Brother of Moses?

Thothmes (sometimes translated as Tutmoses) should have become pharaoh on the death of his father, but he was only a child and his stepmother Hatshepsut saw to it that she was not only the protector of the designated heir to the throne, but she actually usurped that throne for herself.

In view of the fact that the pharaoh was supposed to be the physical son of Ra the sun god, it is indeed surprising that Hatshepsut was able to secure the throne for herself in this way. However, as Thothmes was actually the son of a harem girl it seems probable that the claims of Hatshepsut were enhanced. She herself was of royal blood, and would have been the pharaoh if she had been born male. The fact is, she was able to claim the throne of Egypt and to hold it. Thothmes — her stepson — hated her, and when he eventually

Thothmes III

This is the pharaoh Thothmes III. He had to wait resentfully for many years until his stepmother Hatshepsut died, before he himself became the pharaoh. He and Moses would probably have been boys together in the royal palace.

became pharaoh on her death he had many of her statues and inscriptions destroyed or defaced.

Our picture shows Thothmes III. He and Moses were apparently reared as foster brothers. It is possible that if Moses had not fled from Egypt at the time when he killed an Egyptian overseer, he would have been "taken care of" in a purge anyway. He might well have been a threat to both Hatshepsut and her son Thothmes who became the pharaoh not long after Moses went for his life.

The "original" sky god was Horus. Here he is being suckled by his mother Isis.

Originally the Egyptians Believed in One Great Creator-God

Originally the Egyptians believed in only one great Creator-God. Wallis Budge summarizes some of the evidence and then declares:

> After reading the extracts it is impossible not to conclude that the ideas of the ancient Egyptians about God were of a very exalted character, and it is clear that they made in their minds a sharp distinction between God and the "gods." Several passages in the Theban Recension of the Book of the Dead prove that under the XVIIIth dynasty, about 1600 B.C., they believed that there was a time when the god Tem existed by himself, and that it was he who, by a series of efforts of his mind, created the heavens and the earth, and gods and men, and every creature which has life.

> It was believed that he was self-created and self-existent, and that he was One Only, and the texts . . . state clearly that there was none with him, and that he was quite alone when he arrived

at the decision to create the heavens and the earth, and gods and men. The gods proceeded from his body, and men from the words of his mouth. Here, then, we have One God who was self-created, self-existent, and almighty, who created the universe.[1]

However, as time passed this idea of one great Creator God became lost, with various gods developing from the attributes of that one God. The truth is seen in the Bible, right at the beginning where we are immediately introduced to the Creator God who spoke, and all created matter came into being.

The "original" sky god was Horus, depicted as an outstretched falcon whose two eyes were regarded as the sun and the moon. In early dynastic times this celestial falcon was equated with the king, and so he was a manifestation of Horus. The royal symbol of the winged disc of the falcon incorporated the king, the sun, and the sky.

Osiris, the God of the Underworld

Amenophis in the Likeness of Osiris, the God of the Undeworld

This statue dates to 1540 B.C. Amenophis is represented in the form of the god Osiris. It is at the 11th Dynasty Temple of Nebhepetrie.

Isis was recognized in early Egypt as the original mother goddess, and was credited with restoring her dead husband Osiris to life, and this is tied in with moon worship:

> The phases of the moon were a symbol of life and death, alluding to the death and resurrection of Osiris. The fourteen pieces of Osiris' dismembered body corresponded to the fourteen days of the waning moon. The identification of the moon with the injured eye of Horus played a significant role in myth. In Hellenic times the goddess Isis, whom the Greeks saw as Selene, took a place alongside the more ancient moon deities, Thoth, Khons, Osiris, and Iah, who in the few representations we have of him was shown as a man wearing the royal kilt with the moon disc on his head.[2]

To the Egyptians, Isis became recognized as the mother of the king, being the wife of Osiris and the mother of the god Horus. Isis actually replaced Hathor as the mother goddess.

Even in these early writings it is clear that the persons of the "godhead" are inter-related and confusingly thrown together. Moses would have been taught about these various deities, and at the same time he would have learned of the true God of the Hebrews from his mother who was also employed as his foster mother in the Egyptian palace. As we see in our picture, at times pharaohs such as Amenophis were represented in the likeness of Osiris.

Moses Would Have Learned About "The Lord of Truth"

At Acts 7:22 we read that Moses was instructed in all the wisdom of the Egyptians, and undoubtedly part of his training was a study of the very early *The Book of the Dead*. Here are some of the statements in *The Book of the Dead* about the attributes of the true God, selected from *The Papyrus of Ani*:

A Hymn To Amen-Ra . . . president of all the gods . . . lord of the heavens . . . Lord of Truth . . . maker of men; creator of beasts . . . Ra, whose word is truth, the Governor of the world, the mighty one of valour, the chiefs who made the world as he made himself. His forms are more numerous than those of any god. . . .

Adoration be to thee, O Maker of the Gods, who hast stretched out the heavens and founded the earth! . . . lord of eternity, maker of the everlastingness . . . creator of light. . . .

He heareth the prayer of the oppressed one, he is kind of heart to him that calleth upon him, he delivereth the timid man from the oppressor . . . He is the Lord of knowledge, and Wisdom is the utterance of his mouth.

He maketh the green herb whereon the cattle live, and the staff of life whereon men live. He maketh the fish to live in the rivers, and the feathered fowl in the sky. He giveth life to that which is in the egg.[3]

Amen-Ra, the Great Creator God to the Early Egyptians

Amen-Ra supposedly assumed many forms and his attributes were absorbed by lesser deities. Originally the Egyptians had vague ideas as to the fact that there was originally one great Creator. Again we quote from the Egyptian *Book of the Dead*:

Hail to thee, O thou maker of all these things, thou ONLY ONE. In his mightiness he taketh many forms.

Amen-Ra was the impersonal sun god, and as Moses was instructed in all the wisdom of the Egyptians he would have been told that this great power in the heavens was the original creator and that the pharaoh was the living manifestation of that impersonal power. The truth of one great personal God, Moses would have known from his mother, but not from Egyptian tutors!

It must have been difficult for both Moses and his mother for him to be informed so learnedly by the priests that his own foster mother was a living manifestation of the Amen-Ra the creator. Wallis Budge points out that "after reading the above extracts it is impossible not to conclude that the ideas of the ancient Egyptians about God were of a very exalted character, and it is clear that they made in their minds a sharp distinction between God and the 'gods.' . . . Here then we have one God who was self-created, self-existent, and almighty, who created the universe."

The fact is, Budge sees monotheism as the original Egyptian belief corrupted into polytheism. He argues convincingly that the various attributes of the one great God were transferred to become other lesser gods. He states that, "The truth of the matter seems to me to be that the Egyptian religion never wholly lost the monotheistic element which was in it." He suggests a similarity to the monotheism of the Hebrews.[4] Crude polytheism developed in Egyptian history, with increasing numbers of deities. This is an indirect confirmation of a beginning with monotheism — not "many gods."

Did Moses "Borrow" Monotheism?

It is sometimes stated that Moses simply borrowed the concept of monotheism from his Egyptian background. But it can be clearly seen that Moses' understanding of God is very different from that put forward at any period of ancient Egyptian history. It can be shown just as clearly that no other ancient people thought of God as all-powerful, personally interested in men, and demanding holiness on man's part.

The man from whom Moses is supposed to have borrowed his lofty ideas is the pharaoh Amenhotep IV, who reigned from about 1370-1353 B.C. Somewhere about 1365 B.C. Amenhotep changed his name to Akhenaton (denoting worship of "Aton" the sun disc). It seems that Akhenaton was influenced by the

Amen-Ra, the President of All the Gods

Moses' tutors would have taught him that Amen-Ra was lord of the heavens, the lord of truth and the creator of all things.

The Many Gods of Egypt Supposedly "Evolved" from One Original God

Four of the Egyptian gods as depicted in the British Museum — the baboon; Thoris, the goddess of childbirth; another baboon; and Horus as a falcon.

remarkable woman who was his mother, and he did away with the worship of many gods (i.e. polytheism) so traditional in ancient Egypt. Thus he claimed that the sun god alone, of the recognized deities, should be worshiped, and that he, as the representative of the sun god, should also be worshiped.

On His Death, Akhenaton Was Denounced as a Heretic

This so-called heresy was prevalent in Egypt for about 15 years, and in that time Akhenaton repressed polytheistic worship with great violence, so much so that later generations referred to him as "the criminal of Ahen-taten" — Ahen-taten being the name of his capital city. No doubt there were those who recognized that some teachings Akhenaton put forward had merit in them when compared with the tyranny of the traditional priests of Egypt, but very soon after Akhenaton died, Egypt reverted to polytheism. The

This is Akhenaton from whom Moses supposedly "borrowed" monotheism — but Akhenaton was later than Moses.

Akhenaton with Queen Nefertiti Makes Offerings to the Sun God

The rays from the sun god stream down as though in benediction on the pharaoh, his wife, and his daughter.

sun god became recognized again as simply one of many gods.

Although Akhenaton did talk about the sun as "the god beside whom there is none other," and regarded it as the creator of all things, his concept of deity was greatly removed from that put forward by Moses. The sun disc was simply a vague, impersonal power, necessarily disinterested in the affairs of men, and there is no thought of ethics associated with this worship. In fact, in the implementation of his beliefs there is a great contrast with the ethics and morality associated with the worship of Jehovah.

Akhenaton was putting himself alongside deity: he was the specially favored one. And in rejecting the worship of other gods, at least to some extent he was clearly inspired by self-centered ideas of his own greatness.

Moses, on the other hand, made little of his own greatness. He led his people along the pathway of devotion to the one true god, the Holy God who demanded holiness from each of His people. We can see how different this was from the religious ideas of Pharaoh Akhenaton.

Why Did Moses Flee from Egypt?

We have already seen that Hatshepsut was probably the princess who rescued the infant Moses from the Nile, and she became the only woman pharaoh of Egypt. She might well have turned against Moses because of his non-Egyptian stance when he identified himself with his own slave people. She was a very determined, aggressive woman, and she would hardly have tolerated anti-Egyptian activities, even from a relative.

In addition to all this, instead of being acceptable as a possible successor, Moses might very well have posed a threat to her present leadership. A woman leader in Egypt would not have been without some opposition, and the records about Moses in the Pentateuch make it clear that he was an extremely capable man, and he became an outstanding leader. Very possibly Hatshepsut now saw him as a potential enemy rather than a beloved foster son.

Exodus 2:12 shows that Moses' action was deliberate, and not just an accidental killing. He was emerging as the champion of his people, and presumably there would have been other "straws in the wind." Verse 14 shows that Moses was afraid, and verse 15 tells us he fled from the pharaoh because the pharaoh wanted to kill him. If this was the only incident, we would expect a member of the royal household (Moses) to be able to defend the isolated incident, but Moses wasted no time. He went for his life. Perhaps it was just the opportunity that the pharaoh wanted, to get rid of someone who was now a potential rival for the highest office in the land — which she held.

Exodus 2:23 says the king (ruler) of Egypt died while Moses was in Midian. On our present reconstruction this was Pharaoh Hatshepsut whose picture in stone is before us.

Exodus 18:9-12 indicates that Jethro had a personal experience of the true God Jehovah (YAHWEH). The time came later when Moses was leading his people through the wilderness, that Jethro took a burnt offering and offered it to the Lord.

It is significant that Moses spent 40 years in Midian, and now Jethro would have taught him much. Possibly he was a great influence on Moses who was destined to be a special prophet of the Lord — even pointing on to his death, as in the offering of the Passover Lamb and other Old Testament "types."

Another Statue of the Pharaoh Hatshepsut

Hatshepsut boasted she had removed from Avaris the Asiatics "whom the gods abominate, and earth has carried off their footprints." It would not be surprising that she would despise Moses for siding with the Hebrew slaves.

Moses Becomes a Shepherd in the Land of Midian

Exodus 2:15 tells of Moses going for his life "from the face of pharaoh" and he reached the land of Midian. There he sat by a well, and the seven daughters of Reuel (also known as Jethro) came to feed their sheep. However, when they drew the water the local shepherds came and drove them away.

Once again Moses stood up for the oppressed, as he had done for his brethren in Egypt. He helped the seven young ladies and they were able to water their flock much more quickly than usual. When they came home to their father he asked how it was that they were home so soon. They told him that an Egyptian had delivered them from the local shepherds and then drew water for them and watered their flock. It is interesting to note that these young ladies recognized Moses as an Egyptian. He was very much a product of the Egyptian palace, even though he was at heart a true Hebrew.

Reuel asked the girls where Moses was and why they had not offered him hospitality. They went and invited Moses into the house, "Then Moses was content to live with the man, and he gave Zipporah his daughter to Moses. And she bore him a son, and he called his name Gershom; for he said, "I have been a stranger in a foreign land" (Exod. 2:21-22).

At Exodus 3:1 we find that Moses became a shepherd looking after the flock of Jethro his father-in-law, the priest of Midian — as here depicted. Moses spent 40 years in the Egyptian palace and another 40 years as a shepherd in Midian. There, in relative obscurity, he no doubt "unlearned" much that would have seemed so important to his Egyptian tutors and peers.

Moses, the Shepherd of Midian Was to Become a Great Prophet of the Redeemer Who Would Die

Moses and the Burning Bush

And the Angel of the Lord appeared to him in a flame of fire from the midst of a bush. So he looked, and behold, the bush was burning with fire, but the bush was not consumed.

Then Moses said, "I will now turn aside and see this great sight, why the bush does not burn."

So when the Lord saw that he turned aside to look, God called to him from the midst of the bush and said, "Moses, Moses!" And he said, "Here I am."

Then He said, "Do not draw near this place. Take your sandals off your feet, for the place where you stand is holy ground."

Moreover He said, "I am the God of your father — the God of Abraham, the God of Isaac, and the God of Jacob." And Moses hid his face, for he was afraid to look upon God.

As we go on we find that God was about to send Moses to deliver His people from their affliction in Egypt . . . "for I know their sorrows" (Exod. 3:7).

While watching over the flock of Jethro, Moses came to Horeb, "the Mountain of God."
There the Lord appeared to him in the midst of a bush that was on fire and yet not
consumed by that fire.

"Take Your Sandals Off Your Feet, for the Place Where You Stand Is Holy Ground"

Moses would have been told by his tutors in Egypt about the sacred bull Apis, about the myths of creation involving the four sons of Horus, about the death rituals such as weighing the heart against the feather of truth. Through his mother's teaching he would have rejected it all. Now the truth is burned into his very being . . . at the burning bush God said to Moses, "I AM the God of your father, the God of Abraham, the God of Isaac, and the God of Jacob."

In Exodus 3:5 we read that the Lord told Moses to take the shoes off his feet because he was "standing on holy ground." Moses obeyed and then the Lord revealed to Moses who He was, and what He was about to do to deliver His people from the oppression of the Egyptians.

In Mark 12:26 our Lord reminded the Sadducees of what had been said to Moses at the burning bush, and then He went on to say, "He is not the God of the dead, but the God of the living." Abraham, Isaac, and Jacob were alive in the presence of God.

Jesus said to the Jewish leaders, "Before Abraham was, I Am" (John 8:58). In John's Gospel there are many references to the "I AM" — and indeed this was taken as a title by false gods such as the Egyptian goddess Isis. The "I AM" was the ever-living, self-existent One — the One who had no beginning and no ending. Among other titles that Jesus used is this at John 14:6, "I am the way, the truth, and the life." We have already seen that Moses would have been instructed in the teachings in what we now call *The Book of the Dead* in which the original Egyptian creator-god declared of himself, "I am the truth."

Moses was being given an essential lesson as to the nature of God — the true God, and not the false gods of ancient Egypt. Despite his hesitation, any confusion from Egypt was past. Moses knew that he was in the presence of the Eternal One, the great Creator, the ever-living "I AM." And now Moses was to go to Pharaoh with the command to let God's people depart from Egypt and to be released from slavery.

Taskmaster's Diary

So Moses returned to Egypt where his people were suffering dreadfully under the scourges of their cruel masters.

Pictured here is an Egyptian taskmaster's diary. It reminds us again of the way the taskmasters were so very much in authority over the Hebrews who were now slaves in Egypt. Their lot was dreadful — so different from when Jacob and his family came into Egypt as honored guests. Now they were slaves, longing for deliverance by Jehovah.

When the Lord appeared to Moses in the burning bush He further said:

I have surely seen the oppression of My people who are in Egypt, and have heard their cry because of their taskmasters, for I know their sorrows.

So I have come down to deliver them out of the hand of the Egyptians, and to bring them up from that land to a good and large land, to a land flowing with milk and honey, to the place of the Canaanites and the Hittites and the Amorites and the Perizzites and the Hivites and the Jebusites (Exod. 3:7-8).

This taskmaster's diary makes it clear that details about production were recorded and that the slaves were treated almost like animals. The Bible story breathes the atmosphere of the times.

A taskmaster's diary such as this was an important record. Many of the pharaohs had ambitious building projects, and accurate records were maintained. The names of some slaves were recorded, and so also was the daily tally of bricks. Even excuses for not coming to work were recorded — reminding us of the statement of the pharaoh and the actions of the taskmasters in Exodus 5:8-9:

And you shall lay on them the quota of bricks which they made before. You shall not reduce it. For they are idle. . . . Let more work be laid on the men, that they may labor in it, and let them not regard false words.

It was to these people that Moses came, sent by God. He was that longed-for deliverer, the one who would lead them out towards the Promised Land that God gave to His covenant people.

Papyrus Reeds

We have already seen one use of papyrus reeds. Before us is a clump of papyrus that has been carefully cultivated in modern times on the River Nile. We saw that Moses was put inside an ark made of bulrushes — literally, a papyrus boat. As we consider the culture of Egypt, it is relevant to recognize that "papyrus" is the word from which we get paper. Writing in Egypt was often on these reeds rather than on the clay which was associated with writing in ancient Babylonia.

It is a sad fact that many papyrus documents have been lost by decomposition, and even by deliberate destruction. Nevertheless, a great deal of light has been thrown on life in ancient Egypt from recovered documents, and from tomb inscriptions and other monuments. From such records we are able to glean a great deal of information about the background against which Moses declared his belief in the God of the Hebrews, the One who really was the God of Truth.

Papyrus reeds grew plentifully in Egypt in ancient times — though not today. The ark of bulrushes for Moses would have been made of papyrus reeds. A great deal of writing in ancient Egypt was on papyrus sheets.

Some of those early Egyptian teachings had elements of truth in them — such as the belief that at death the heart of the deceased was weighed against the feather of truth. This did demonstrate their belief in life after death and recognized the need to adhere to a given divine standard of truth.

Brickmaking in Modern Egypt

Dr. Clifford Wilson took this photograph of a brickmaker making bricks in the general area of Thebes, out from Luxor in Egypt. He was quite willing to demonstrate his trade so long as bucksheesh was paid! After he had formed the brick, the brickmaker would add it to his pile of similar bricks that were laid out in neat rows. Thus they would be sun dried in the very hot conditions of Egypt.

Notice that the straw is contained within these modern Egyptian bricks. It would seem that the method demonstrated here is remarkably similar to that of ancient times, with similar results. They were — and are — remarkably effective.

Mud bricks are again popular today, not only in the so-called poorer countries but in many western countries as well. Straw is not necessarily used as the binder these days, being replaced by chemical bonding materials.

We have already seen that the people of Moses had become slaves. They were forced to make bricks for the massive building projects of the pharaoh, with decreasing quantities of straw but still with brutal insistence on the production of a full quota each day.

Mud Brick from Egypt

There are various indications from Egypt that the taskmasters were extremely severe on their slaves. One bowl depicts a taskmaster with two slaves prostrate before him. He appears to be holding the hair of both of them while their eyes are bound. He himself has a club uplifted in his right hand.

The so-called *Papyrus Anastasi* from Egypt tells of an Egyptian officer who was supervising construction in the land of Goshen (which was where the Israelites were slaves). He writes, "I do not have any materials and help. There is no one to make bricks, there is no straw in this area" — somewhat similar to the plight of the Hebrews in Egypt, as described in Exodus 5:7-12.

In some excavated buildings the quantity of straw decreased as the building progressed, and that may be a reflection of the fact that Israelites were involved. However, the dating is not precise and we cannot say for sure that these inferior bricks were made by the Hebrews. Other people were also used as slaves, including large numbers of captives from Canaan.

The Bible record about the slaves in Egypt certainly fits the known Egyptian background.

A Brick from Ancient Egypt

This brick in the collection of the Australian Institute of Archaeology was made by slaves in Egypt. It is so poorly preserved that it needs to be protected in cottonwool, with a wooden frame on the outside.

Gods of Ancient Egypt

These are more of the gods of Egypt. At the time of the "ten plagues" many Egyptian gods were discredited. As we go through the judgments, on every occasion an important god of Egypt was shown to be without power.

We have begun to see the pharaoh's reaction when Moses asked for favors for the Hebrew slaves. An important aspect of the pharaoh's reaction is his own belief in his divinity. Notice the gods in this picture. They are typical of the gods of ancient Egypt: they literally numbered in the thousands. Each village would have a shrine dedicated to its local deity, and the worship of that god was supposed to be a unifying factor for the community.

The pharaoh himself was considered to be a chief god, as an incarnation of Horus and Ra. He was a god in his own right, yet he was also the manifestation on earth of the chief deified power, the sun.

Some gods were more important than others, with specialized activities. The scribal god was supposed to be the lord of divine words, and was given credit for inventing hieroglyphics. Thus he was the god of learning in a general way. Another was Sobec, the god of the waters.

There were goddesses as well as gods. Thus, the cow goddess Hathor was the goddess of love, and Sekhmet of Memphis was a fire goddess who delighted to annihilate her enemies — a contrast with Hathor, the goddess of love and joy. Heqt the frog goddess was supposed to control fertility (very ineffectively even for frogs at the time of the plagues!) — they overran the whole of Egypt, as Exodus 8:13-14 shows.

For the Egyptians there were multitudes of lesser gods, demons, and evil creatures who could hurt or injure men as they chose.

The Pharaoh Was Worshiped

This is an unnamed Amen-Ra image from Egypt in the possession of Dr. Clifford Wilson. It is a statuette about five inches high, and it is cast in bronze. All pharaohs were supposed to be the present living manifestation of Ra the sun god, and all were worshiped.

In size this is similar to some of the household gods from ancient Sumer — the "gods" came in many sizes and shapes, with interchange between cities a common practice. As a particular god was associated with a village or a city, there were times when it was taken to other nearby towns to share in worship and festivity, especially in times of peace.

Sometimes temples for those other gods were built in nearby cities, and a whole pantheon of gods and demi-gods was honored. Other humans were deified at times, as with Imhotep, the medical practitioner who was the chief minister of Pharaoh Zozer. He grew in legendary stature, and was eventually venerated as the god of wisdom and medicine.

The pharaoh at the time of the Exodus sneered and asked, "Who is the Lord? . . . I do not know the Lord" (Exod. 5: 2). Was not he himself the true god, the manifestation of the sun god Ra? However, Jehovah decreed, "Against all the gods of Egypt I will execute judgment" (Exod. 12:12). This judgment included the foolish pharaoh and he died when he opposed the true God.

Weighing a Heart Against a Feather

Egyptian inscriptions are largely related to religious matters and aspects of funerary interest. One of the most important collections of texts (with many variations) is *The Book of the Dead*.

Before us is the Ani Papyrus, it being the longest text of this type from this particular period: it is 76

Egypt worshiped many gods, and this scene from the Ani Papyrus of The Book of the Dead *(about 1300 B.C.) points to their belief that there would be a day of judgment when the heart with its sins would be weighed against the feather of truth.*

feet long and 15 inches wide. The original is now in the British Museum. Rolls of inscribed papyrus like this were often buried with the dead in Egypt, including prayers and hymns so that the person being buried could overcome the terrors of the underworld and eventually arrive at the "fields of peace."

Here Ani is being conducted into the presence of the gods, who can be seen seated as assessors at the top half of the picture. His heart will be weighed against the feather of truth, and the balances must be exactly level. It is not possible for the heart to be heavier than the feather, for that would suggest that something could be greater than the truth to which the feather pointed. On the other hand, the heart could not weigh less than the feather, for that would mean that sin was on the heart, weighing it down. Therefore, the scales had to be exactly level, with the heart weighing just the same as the feather.

The Heart and the Feather Again

At times an inscription would be made on a mummy to the effect that the heart had already been weighed against the feather, and that the scales were exactly level. It seems that a bribe was paid to the priests so that the deceased person could pass the test, and be conducted into the next stage of eternity. Otherwise he would be devoured by the crocodile goddess, Amit, who can be seen at the right hand of the picture, hopefully anticipating that the heart will be tossed to her because it does not weigh up to the standard of truth. Thoth, the recording god, is seen in front of the crocodile goddess.

The levels are exactly level, the 11 assessor gods are deceived, the crocodile god goes hungry (not able to devour the heart), and the deceased takes his place with those who are enjoying the life after death.

These religious ceremonials often have a measure of truth with them. The Christian teaching is that Jesus is the truth. We have forgiveness of sins, the balancing of the scales being possible because He has taken the penalty of our sins upon himself.

It is appointed unto man once to die and after that the judgment (Heb. 9:27), but that judgment is not associated with the grotesque and magical gods of Egypt. It is according to the standards of Jehovah, the one pure and Holy God of truth. It is He, and He only, who can declare that the sinner is forgiven and can be given eternal life, the abundant life that Jesus spoke of. It is very different from the Scripture that says, "Do not be deceived, God is not mocked; for whatever a man sows, that he will also reap" (Gal. 6:7).

Once again we are reminded that Moses would have known of these teachings, but it becomes clear in the Pentateuch that a higher standard is presented — the writings of Moses constantly bear within them the imprint of the finger of God.

Life After Death

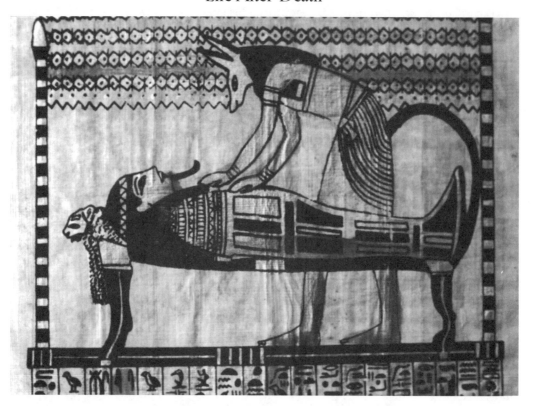

This particular picture is from the British Museum and it shows Anubis, the jackal-headed god, performing the ceremony of "opening the mouth." This was supposed to make it possible for the person who had died to be able to eat, breathe, smell, hear, and speak in the next life.

As we consider the implications of weighing the heart of a deceased person against the feather of truth it becomes clear that the early Egyptians believed that there was life after death. Because of this belief, they embalmed the bodies of departed kings, officials, and even relatives and, if they could afford it, this process was carried out using the mineral natron which was supposed to protect the body against decay.

Eventually it was put inside a coffin, but not before a number of important rituals had been carried out. The jackal-headed god Anubis is shown in many Egyptian tomb paintings (and others on papyrus) overseeing these proceedings in his role as the guide of human souls into the hereafter.

Once again there is a glimmer of truth in these Egyptian practices. No animal or bird ever buried its dead or attempted to preserve the body for a future life. Nor did such creatures ever put food, clothing, weapons, or household utensils and furniture alongside a departed "colleague" so that they would be provided for in the hereafter. Man, who is made in the image of God alone, shows his belief in life to come, and in an ongoing relationship with divinity.

Horus and His Four Sons

By the time of Moses, Egyptian religion was very complex, and there were even several gods who at times are given prominence as being the chief of the gods — including Ptah of Memphis, Amun of Thebes, and Re (Ra) or Atum the sun god. Others who came into prominence included Horus and his four sons.

Horus and his four sons are each armed with a knife as they stand in the presence of the gods Osiris and Serapis. Notice the man with the head of an animal bound by his arms, with knives stuck in his body. He represents a conquered god.

Professor Kenneth Kitchen writes in *The Illustrated Bible Dictionary*:

> The nearest thing to a truly national religion was the cult of Osiris and his cycle (with his wife, Isis, and son, Horus). The story of Osiris had great human appeal: the good king, murdered by his wicked brother Seth, becoming ruler of the realm of the dead and triumphing in the person of his posthumous son and avenger Horus, who, with the support of his mother Isis, gained his father's kingship on earth. The Egyptian could identify himself with Osiris the revivified in his kingdom of the hereafter; Osiris' other aspect, as a god of vegetation, linking with the annual rise of the Nile and consequent rebirth of life, combined powerfully with his funerary aspect in Egyptian aspirations.[5]

There are many indications that the Egyptians believed in resurrection and the hereafter. Thus, our picture shows Horus and his four sons, each of them being armed with a knife as they stand before the gods Osiris and Serapis. The Egyptian practice was to place embalmed organs of deceased persons inside four canopic jars. The four stoppers on the jars represented the four sons of Horus.

Osiris was the god of the underworld and the Nile was supposed to be his lifeblood. When the Nile was turned into blood the river was clearly not the lifeblood of Osiris, for it became a blood bath. Thus, the second-most important god of Egypt was seriously discredited. (At times he was even placed above Ra the sun god.)

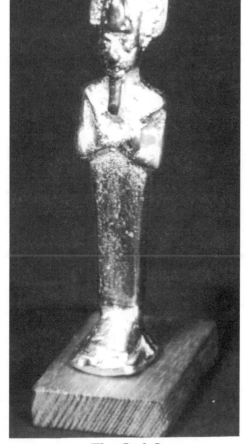

The God Osiris

Osiris

There were grotesque intrigues in the company of the gods, and the wicked god Seth had Osiris killed by 72 of his henchmen. Now we again meet Isis. She was both the wife and the sister of Osiris. She went in search of her husband and in two separate instances where Seth first killed and then mutilated the body of Osiris, she was able to recover the body.

Osiris was brought back to life, and ruled in the West as the king of the blessed dead. He was regarded as the god of the underworld and of the afterlife, being second only to Ra the sun god. The Egyptians believed that because Osiris had been restored to life, they too could hope for a blessed life beyond the grave.

There are various magical formulae and spells associated with the gaining of life after death, but they would be effective only if the deceased had lived the virtuous(?) sort of life that Osiris had lived.

In Exodus 12:12 we read, "Against all the gods of Egypt I will execute judgment." It can be shown that every one of the ten plagues was a judgment against specific leading gods of Egypt. The true God was vindicated, for the forces of evil were shown to be without power when they dared to oppose the omnipotent God, Jehovah of the Hebrews.

Hatmehyt, the Fish Goddess of the Nile

We have said that each of the plagues would have seriously discredited at least one of the leading gods of Egypt. Thus, when the River Nile was turned into blood, this was a serious discrediting of a number of leading gods. We have already seen that Osiris was shown to be without power, and Hapi, the god of the Nile, was also seriously discredited. So also was Hatmehyt, and she also did not escape judgment. Her symbol was a fish, and all the fish of the Nile died.

Our picture is a reminder of the importance of the Nile for Egyptian fishermen, from the pharaoh on his throne right down to the humble field worker who needed the fish as part of his sustenance. Men, women, children, fish — and even the birds — were drastically affected when the Nile turned into blood.

This series of judgments was one of the most dramatic demonstrations in all Scripture that there was only one true God. In the time of Elijah there was a similar manifestation of divine power when the prophets of Baal were discredited and Baal was shown to be without power. So now the many gods of Egypt were shown for what they were — corrupted distortions of the true God.

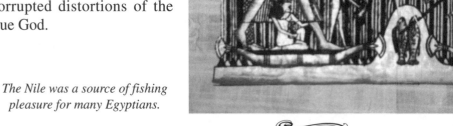

The Nile was a source of fishing pleasure for many Egyptians.

The Plaque of Frogs

The second judgment, that of frogs, is recorded in Exodus 8:5-14. On this occasion the frog goddess Heqt was seriously discredited for she was supposed to be the goddess of fertility, and the patroness of the midwives. She is presented in Egyptian paintings with the body of a woman and the head of a frog. Yet Heqt could not even control the fertility of frogs! Heqt was so important to the Egyptians that in one ancient picture she is shown helping the god Anubis reconstruct the body of Osiris which — as we have seen — the god Seth had hacked to pieces.

Heqt was supposed to be the goddess of fertility, but she could not control the fertility even of frogs!

The Bible record is quite dramatic. The Lord told Moses to instruct Aaron to stretch forth his hand with his rod over the streams, the rivers, and the ponds of Egypt. When Aaron obeyed, the frogs came up and covered the whole land. However, the Egyptian priests were able to do the same with their enchantments — but it is clear that they were unable to cause the judgment to cease. Only Aaron, under God, could do that.

It was then that the pharaoh called for Moses and asked that he entreat the Lord to take the frogs away — and the pharaoh promised he would then let the people go that they might sacrifice to the Lord. So that the pharaoh would know that it was indeed the hand of the Lord, Moses asked the pharaoh when the plague should stop and the pharaoh answered, "Tomorrow." Moses agreed to this so that the pharaoh would know that there "is no one like the Lord our God" (Exod. 8:10).

The Frogs Are Removed

Images such as this frog were common in Egypt, as were images dedicated to many other creatures that were worshiped as gods.

Moses declared to the pharaoh that the frogs would be taken from the houses and from among the Egyptian people, remaining only in the area of the river. Then Moses and Aaron went out from the pharaoh, and Moses cried earnestly to the Lord that the frogs would be removed.

So the Lord did according to the word of Moses. And the frogs died out of the houses, out of the courtyards, and out of the fields.

They gathered them together in heaps, and the land stank.

But when Pharaoh saw that there was relief, he hardened his heart and did not heed them, as the Lord had said (Exod. 8:13-15).

Egyptian ladies often made offerings to Heqt to protect them in childbirth, and to give them their desired offspring.

Critics sometimes ask why it is stated at times, "But the Lord hardened Pharaoh's heart and he would not let them go" (Exod. 10:27). The answer is that Pharaoh first hardened his own heart, as we read in the incident of the frogs (Exod. 8:15). Ultimately it is true that God is "the First Cause," and the Hebrew people themselves could attribute all activities to God — thus we read that Satan tempted David to number the people, but we also read that this action is also attributed to God.

(See 2 Sam. 24:1 where we read that the Lord moved David to number Israel and Judah. Then go to 1 Chron. 21:1-3 where we read that Satan provoked David to number Israel. David did so even though Joab told him that this would be the cause of trespass.)

So with Pharaoh — the Lord hardened his heart, but only after Pharaoh had decided for himself.

The Sacred Land of Egypt Was Defiled

We read of the next plague or judgment at Exodus 8:16-19. Once again, Aaron was to stretch out his rod and now he was to smite the dust of the land so that it would become lice throughout all the land of Egypt. That whole land was supposedly sacred to the gods, and now it became unclean.

Our picture is of a series of pyramids at Giza outside modern Cairo. People often ask if the Hebrews built these pyramids when they were slaves in Egypt, but in fact they had been built for hundreds of years before the time of Joseph. Mainly they were burial places for pharaohs, on what was then the west side of the Nile River, because it was believed that the pharaoh was about to rejoin the chariot of the gods from whom he was descended. In other words, the pharaoh was supposed to re-enter the sun after his own death. His burial in one of the pyramids made it an especially sacred spot.

Now the whole land — pyramids and all — was suffering the judgment of God as the dust was turned to lice. The corn crops such as the one in this picture would have been ruined, for one practical effect of

Today Egypt is typified by the famous pyramids, and it was also so in the days of Moses. The pyramids were built long before his time. Our picture shows a corn crop near the sacred Nile — and all this area was to know the judgment of the lice.

this judgment was that the food supply was drastically reduced.

God was using dramatic "visual aids" — powerful teaching methodology. The foolish pharaoh would not act appropriately, and the judgments necessarily continued.

Man and Beast Were Equally Affected

This scene from ancient Egypt is of an inspection of cattle. Not only the land, but living creatures, also were now afflicted by the plague of lice — and the priests were powerless.

We have seen that Aaron smote the dust of the land when he stretched out his hand with the rod, "And it became lice in man and in beast" (Exod. 8:17).

Much of the economy of Egypt depended on the work force out in the fields, and now the people would feel the effect of this stated judgment of God as the so-called sacred land of Egypt itself came under the judgment of the God against whom the pharaoh had sneered, "Who is the Lord, that I should obey His voice to let Israel go? I do not know the Lord, nor will I let Israel go" (Exod. 5:2).

Moses had told the pharaoh of the true God, Yahweh (Jehovah), but the pharaoh had rejected the teaching of Moses, for was not he himself the true son of the great Ra, the primary god of the heavens? So he had boasted, "I do not know Him." But despite the pharaoh's arrogance, the priest/magicians had now to acknowledge that this was the finger of God (Exod. 8:19).

This becomes more understandable when we find that an expression in Egyptian magical texts refers to the "finger of Seth," an expression which had its origin in the myth of Seth fighting Horus for world domination. Similarly we read of "the finger of Thoth." He was regarded as the god who was especially the foe of the sun god Ra.

Now the pharaoh was warned by his own priests, "this is the finger of God." But still he refused to let the people go.

Khepira, the Beetle God

This is Khepira the beetle god, another Egyptian deity. One of the ten judgments involved "swarms of flies" — but "of flies" is in italics in the Authorized Version of the Bible. The word "arob" at Exodus 8:21-24 has been translated "swarm" or "flies." It applies to insects in general, and would include flies. In the British Museum there are ornaments of flies which were supposed to make it possible for the wearer to ascend to heaven.

The Bible talks about the flies but actually the word is "swarms," and the beetle god was included in that description. Exodus 12:12 states, "Against all the gods of Egypt I will execute judgment." The prophesied judgments came to pass.

Also, in chapter 76 of *The Book of the Dead,* honor is given to the bird fly who was supposedly able to bring a man to heaven.

The word also probably included beetles, and it has long been known that Khepira, the beetle god, was widely worshiped; he was recognized as the god of the resurrection. But Khepira was also powerless: only the true God of heaven is the God of the resurrection.

The Disease Upon Cattle

The fifth judgment was the disease upon cattle as recorded in Exodus 9:1-7. Until this time the plagues had brought physical discomfort, but now property was more dramatically affected. Many tombs

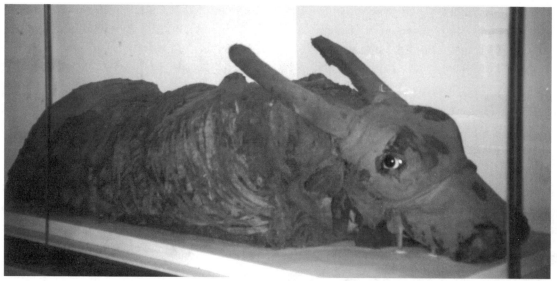

An Embalmbed Bull

Many such animals were embalmed — they were gods in the flesh and skins of animals!

of ancient Egypt depict flocks and herds, and this judgment against the cattle was a very real evidence of the divine power which was demonstrated through Moses and Aaron. Apis the bull god was among the gods discredited, and so also was Hathor the goddess of love, so often depicted as a cow.

Many pictures from ancient Egypt make it clear that the well-being of animals was tremendously important. There are scenes of men with animals, plowing the land for crops.

Sometimes even the women were shown guiding the plow, and now for Moses to declare that all the animals would be struck with disease was a serious threat indeed. Not only that, but the disease on the cattle was to be restricted to those of the Egyptians, with the Israelite cattle not affected.

Many of these animals were sacred — the bull, the cow, and the ram — and the problem of embalming many of the cattle associated with the temples would have been very great indeed. Great cemeteries of embalmed animals have been found in ancient Egypt.

Through this judgment the priesthood and the gods themselves were seriously discredited; and, in the case of the priests, they were seriously inconvenienced and overworked.

"I Sent the Hornet Before You"

The bee was part of the symbolism on the cartouche of Thutmose III. It was possibly a symbol of the Egyptian army.

I sent the hornet before you, which drove them out from before you, also the two
kings of the Amorites; but not with your sword or with your bow (Josh. 24:12).

Joshua had to remind his people that though they had fought the enemy, it was really God who had won the victory for them (Exod. 23:28). The hornet was known in these early biblical times as a viciously stinging wasp, and possibly the term is used to symbolize the fear which God sent among the Canaanites in advance of the Israelite armies.

It has been argued that the bee was a symbol of the Egyptian army. There are various presentations of this carved into stone, as this picture reminds us. Possibly God used the Egyptian army to "soften up" the

Another Bee Symbol from Egypt

The campaigns of Thutmose III into Canaan are well-documented. It seems that the bee was part of his symbolism, and of Amenhotep II after him. Possibly God used his armies to "soften up" the Canaanites before the Children of Israel came against them after the wilderness wanderings.

Canaanites and other inhabitants of the Promised Land.

We do not always know where the symbolic and the literal combine in Scripture, and it is a fact that the Holy Spirit of God will at times use symbolism as well as literal fact to convey His truth. In this case the important fact is that the Israelites were to recognize that it was God who went before them.

The Armies of Thutmuse III and Amenhotep II

It is an established fact of Egyptian history that Pharaoh Amenhotep II destroyed many Canaanite cities immediately before and during the times that the Israelites were wandering in the wilderness. Amenhotep II apparently became the pharaoh immediately after the Israelites left Egypt, with his father and his own son having been killed in Egypt while he himself was actively campaigning in Canaan. As we have seen above, the Lord possibly meant the Egyptian armies, especially of Thutmose III and Amenhotep II, when He referred to the fact that He had used the "hornet" as part of His method to destroy the people of Canaan. As we have seen above, possibly the hornet or bee symbol of Thutmoses III is here referred to.

A further point about Thutmose III and Amenhotep II is made by Professor Jack Finegan in *Light from the Ancient East* when he writes:

It may be that he was co-regent with his father for a year or so.[6]

This would mean that it was the first-born son of the co-regent pharaoh who died, as well as the boy's grandfather, the pharaoh who died in the pursuit of the Israelites. It would seem that Amenhotep II did not die at the time of the plague because he was out of Egypt campaigning in Canaan: the judgment was on the first-born in Egypt (Exod. 11:5), and so the absent Amenhotep was not so judged.

Notice in passing that Psalm 105:30 refers to the KINGS (plural) of Egypt at this time. This aptly describes Thothmes III and Amenhotep II, with co-regent Amenhotep's first-born son, the prince who died.

History shows that Amenhotep was especially revengeful by the large number of executions immediately after he returned from campaigning at the time of his father's death. It is possible that in his fury he was attempting to avenge the deaths of both his father and his son.

Thutmose III: The Pharaoh of the Exodus?

Pharaoh Thutmose III of the 18th Dynasty had two splendid red granite obelisks erected in front of the temple of Ra in Heliopolis ("Sun City"). One of these obelisks is now on the Thames embankment in London; the other is in Central Park in New York. On those obelisks is an inscription in which Thutmose describes himself as "Lord of Heliopolis." He also undertook building operations at nearby Memphis, which would have been well-known to Moses.

In personal lecture notes, archaeology researcher Professor Dr. William Shea gives compelling evidence to show that Thutmose III reigned from 1501-1447 B.C. Thutmose III's death can be equated with the Exodus and, indeed, close to an actual day —March 17, 1447 B.C. He apparently died at the right time of the year to coincide with the Passover — "only 10 days after the Exodus according to the lunar calendar, and 14 days after it according to the Egyptian civil calendar."

There is an interesting problem about the supposed body of Thutmose III which lies in the mummy room at the Cairo Museum. Exodus clearly states that he died in the Sea of Reeds:

> Then the waters returned and covered the chariots, the horsemen, and all the army of Pharaoh that came into the sea after them. Not so much as one of them remained (Exod. 14:28).

> For the horses of Pharaoh went with his chariots and his horsemen into the sea, and the Lord brought back the waters of the sea upon them. But the children of Israel went on dry land in the midst of the sea (Exod. 15:19).

It is very interesting to put this alongside another report, this time relating to x-rays of the mummy taken by the Orthodontics Department of the University of Michigan, indicating that the supposed pharaoh was a man of about 40-45 years.

Thutmose III

Accepting the "early" date for the Exodus (about 1447 B.C.) Thutmose III was the pharaoh of the Exodus. It seems that both he and his grandson died at the time of the Exodus from Egypt. (Co-regent Amenhotep II was campaigning in Canaan.)
Our picture is from the British Museum.

Dr. Shea comments on the facts given above:

> This is quite extraordinary in view of the fact that his inscriptions run to year 53, and that he was an infant at least, if not older when he came to the throne . . . From this evidence at least there is a possibility that this was a substituted mummy — i.e., the body was not really recovered in the Red Sea.

Apparently this dismembered body (for so it is) was not that of Thutmose III, for no old man over 80 would show in modern x-rays as approximately half that age. Probably secrecy surrounded the identity of the person buried as Thutmose III.

His "grave" was the Sea of Reeds. However, the priests would need to have someone embalmed as the pharaoh, for he was supposed to be a manifestation of Ra the sun god. He must therefore be buried with appropriate honors on the west side of the Nile. However, if the pharaoh was indeed buried beneath the Sea of Reeds (Red Sea), any other body would do so long as it was properly embalmed in secrecy.

One of the Egyptians troops recovered from the Sea of Reeds would be quite suitable for this, and the modern x-ray pictures indicate that such a replacement did in fact take place — presumably of an Egyptian soldier washed up from the Sea of Reeds.

The Goddess Hathor Protects the Man-god

Hathor the goddess of love was often depicted as a cow. Here she is shown on the side of a massive statue of Thutmose III, the probable pharaoh of the Exodus.

The Great Pyramid and the Sphinx

The "Pyramid Age" is now dated to about 200 years for their total construction. This included those at Giza and many others stretching as far away as Khartoum. Early Egyptian dates have notoriously come down in the last 50 years, and that process might well continue.

There is an interesting legend about the sphinx, concerning a dream sequence by a prince who could be the next pharaoh (Thutmose IV). The legend is that a voice came to the young prince from the sand at the sphinx, telling him that if he would uncover it from the sand, he himself would be pharaoh.

The Great Pyramid and the Sphinx at Giza

This is the Great Pyramid of Cheops (Khurfu) and the sphinx at Giza, outside Cairo. Joseph and Moses would have looked on this pyramid many times, for it was ancient before he came to Egypt. It was not built by Hebrew slaves: pyramids were constructed as burial sites for pharaohs.

The Sphinx at Giza

This is the sphinx that was in the same general area as the Great Pyramid. Moses would possibly have looked on this in his time in Egypt. The sphinx motif of a winged lion and human head is well-known in ancient records.

It seems that he was the second son of the then-ruler, and this would fit the fact that the first son actually died when the judgment of God was visited on Egypt.

As already shown (in *Light from the Ancient East*), Professor Jack Finegan suggests that possibly Thutmose III and Amenhotep II were co-regents before the old king died. If so, the pharaoh's son who died was possibly the son of the co-regent (absent while campaigning in Canaan), as well as being the grandson of the aged pharaoh. In either case he would have been regarded as divine, a manifestation in human form of Ra the sun god.

The Sphinx at Giza Outside Cairo

The famous inscription on the paws of the sphinx tells of a younger son of Amenhotep II (Amenophis II) becoming pharaoh, and this fits the time of the Exodus. This younger son (Thutmose IV, sometimes translated as Thothmes IV) was supposedly rewarded for removing the sand from the Sphinx. He allegedly obeyed the instructions given in a dream, and became the pharaoh.

From J.H. Breasted's well-known *History of Egypt*, the following quotation is relevant:

> Some scholars long suspected . . . that Thutmosis IV was not the eldest son of his father. The contents of the famous Sphinx stele set up during Thutmosis' reign, seems to suggest that prior to the Divine revelation recounted on that monument, he was not expecting to succeed to the throne.

> On the other hand, the inscription in Tomb 64 refers to him specifically as "king's eldest son." Are we here faced with evidence of family strife in the household of Amenophis II (= Amenhotep II)? Was there a struggle for the throne among the sons of the king? And did Thutmosis IV attempt to justify his seizure of the throne by later asserting that he was in fact the elder son of Amenophis II? Or does the appellative signify only that for a short time before his father's death, Dhutmose had the distinction of being "oldest surviving son"?[7]

It seems that Thutmose IV (sometimes spelled as Dhutmose) eventually became pharaoh because his older brother died in infancy at the time of Israel's exodus.

A Dream Sequence in Granite

The young prince who became Pharaoh Thutmose IV was supposedly asleep in the area outside what we call Cairo today. The Great Pyramid was visible, but the Sphinx was not, having been buried by the encroaching sand of the desert.

A dream sequence was recorded on this granite stele between the paws of the sphinx at Giza. The god Harmakhis supposedly promised the young prince Thutmose that he would become pharaoh if he uncovered the sphinx from the sand.

According to legend, the god Harmakhis appeared to Thutmose in a dream and told him that if he would uncover the Sphinx from the sand the throne of Egypt would eventually be his. Such a possibility seemed unlikely, for Thutmose was not the eldest son of his father, the Pharaoh Amenhotep II.

However, Thutmose eventually did become king: apparently his older brother died in infancy. The information about the dream was recorded on a granite stele and put between the paws of the Sphinx.

The dates and the limited information available fit the possibility of that older brother having died at the time of the Exodus from Egypt. Instead of being worshiped as the next manifestation of Ra the sun god, he died according to the pronounced judgment of God against "all the gods of Egypt" (Exod. 12:12).

Pharaoh Thutmose IV

This is a statue in bronze of Pharaoh Thutmose IV. It is about six inches high, and was made by the so-called "lost wax" process. This process was described in *The British Museum Book of Ancient Egypt*:

A model of the object was first fashioned in bees-wax and coated in clay pierced by holes so that when it was heated the wax melted and ran out leaving a hardened clay mould into which the molten metal was introduced through the holes.[8]

While there is still some doubt about the dates for various pharaohs, it has been remarkable how dates have come down and are able to be correlated with biblical data.

This "dream sequence" about Thutmose IV is in that category. The clues given in the Bible fit in ways that are astonishing when put alongside previous secular indifference or even skepticism.

These include the fact of two pharaoh's as co-regent, Moses being known by name to the pharaoh, Moses' very acceptance by palace officials, and an eldest Egyptian son who died and his replacement by another son whose "eldest son" status has some mystery about it.

The Bible records breathe the atmosphere of the times.

The Preservation of the Law of Moses

The Jewish boy carrying this copy of the law of Moses (the "Torah"—"Teaching") is undergoing his Bar-Mitzvah ceremony: for religious purposes he is now recognized as an adult male. Orthodox Jews have great respect for the law of Moses.

The Law of Moses Today

We have seen that a dream inscription dating close to Moses' time was found between the paws of the Sphinx at Giza. Many other Egyptian writings — even by slaves —date to Moses' time, and earlier.

The original law of Moses is not in existence today, but it has been faithfully copied through the centuries. Among other evidences, the findings of the Dead Sea Scrolls make that clear. Right through the centuries religious leaders of Israel have regarded the law of Moses as a final court of appeal. In Jerusalem today there are scholars and students who spend countless hours studying the Torah, clause by clause, and even letter by letter. (One group does so in the building beneath the so-called "Tomb of David.")

The ten commandments in the law of Moses. . . they are unique — and bear within them "the imprint of the finger of God."

The Ten Commandments

The Torah is central in the Bar Mitzvah ceremony whereby on becoming 13 a Jewish boy is confirmed as an adult male in Israel. In this picture at the Western ("Wailing") Wall in Jerusalem, the boy carrying the copy of the Torah is undergoing the ceremony. The boy on his immediate left (or right, looking at the picture) has just kissed the Torah. That respect has continued from the times of Moses to the present. (An optional ceremony for girls is called Bet Mitzvah.)

The Law of Moses is a Unity!

"But" — said the critics, "There were no law codes as early as Moses!"

Unfortunately that false criticism is still hurled at the Pentateuch, the first five books of Moses. We shall see that a number of early law codes are known, and some date to hundreds of years before the time of Moses.

We have already seen that Moses was a highly educated man, and he would have been acquainted with scholarly writings that included cuneiform as well as hieroglyphic writings.

Under God, he was just the right man to lead his people into an appreciation of the mind of God as He gave to His people the most wonderful set of laws that the world had ever seen.

And Jesus and the New Testament writers accepted the great truth that "the law came by Moses" (John 1:17).

A Law Code Near Baghdad

This is the law code from the city of Eshnunna, a few miles outside Baghdad. The original is in the Baghdad Museum, and it dates to about 1900 B.C. Not only was there writing long before Moses' time, but there were also high-class law codes.

From secular records now excavated, we know that even slaves in Egypt inscribed all sorts of information on the walls where they worked. Instead of claiming that it is unreasonable to believe that Moses

Moses' Law Code Was Superior

This law code had clear similarities to the code of Moses in everyday matters, but Moses' code was greatly superior in regard to morals and spiritual realities.

wrote the Pentateuch, the first five books of the Bible, it is unreasonable to suggest that such a compilation from his hands was unlikely.

This law code — and others such as the Code of Hammurabi of Babylon — makes it clear that the laws of Moses were not first written up many hundreds of years after his time, as was so commonly argued before other ancient law codes were recovered.

We mention in passing that the Decalogue itself, the Ten Commandments, is unknown anywhere else in ancient writings. Those Ten Commandments uniquely bear within them the imprint of the finger of God.

The Law Code of the City of Eshnunna

The city of Eshnunna itself is now Tell Asmar, a few miles east of Baghdad. The kingdom flourished about 2000 B.C., and its law code (depicted here) is earlier than that of the famous Hammurabi who lived about 1700 B.C. Tell Asmar was excavated by the Oriental Institute of the University of Chicago, and its prized code is in the Baghdad Museum. It dealt with everyday matters such as rates of wages to be paid, and responsibilities to employees, wives, and slaves. Some penalties for misdemeanors varied dramatically according to social status.

Against that background it is highly relevant to consider the divine standards of the law of Moses: "And what great nation is there that has such statutes and righteous judgments as are in all this law which I set before you this day?" (Deut. 4:8).

Many so-called western countries have utilized much of the principles of the Decalogue in their national laws. If that were true worldwide, and properly upheld, there would be a much higher standard of righteousness and justice. Moses' laws were divinely instituted.

The Code of Hammurabi

Here Shamash the sun god is supposedly giving laws to Hammurabi, the king of Babylon. Possibly the best-known of ancient law codes (apart from that of Moses) is this one of Hammurabi of Babylon, dating to about 1700 B.C. It was found in 1901 at Susa (the biblical Shushan of the Book of Esther) in ancient Persia. It had

Hammurabi's Code dated to about 1700 B.C., well before Moses. Critics said that Moses could not have had such an "advanced" law code, but several other law codes have now been recovered from before his time. His is spiritually unique.

been taken there from Babylon by raiding Elamites. It was a slab approximately seven feet high and six feet in circumference.

It seems probable that copies of this famous code were displayed at various centers so that men could hire a scribe and learn their rights. It had 282 statutes, and they were mainly concerned with civil and criminal law. They dealt with such subjects as witchcraft, bribery, theft, burglary, kidnapping, the duties of public officers, family relations, responsibilities in marriage, adoption, fees to be charged by surgeons, the branding of slaves — and much more.

Although the code of Moses was greatly superior in many ways to the Code of Hammurabi (e.g., he did not condone incest), the similarities make it clear that the legal writings in the Pentateuch are indeed set against the backgrounds and times of Moses, as is claimed in the Bible.

In earlier times it was believed that Hammurabi was the Amraphel of Genesis 14:1, but it is now recognized that Amraphel lived well before the time of Hammurabi.

The Samaritan Pentateuch

Possibly Israel's northern kingdom would have had copies of the law of Moses, for the tabernacle was from time to time in the northern area — one example being that it was in Shiloh at the time of Eli about 1050 B.C. (1 Sam. 4:3). Psalm 78:60 and Jeremiah 7:12, 14, and 25:6 indicate that Shiloh was long remembered as the resting place of the tabernacle. During part of David's reign it was at Gibeon (1 Chron. 1:21, 29).

Until the division at the death of Solomon there would have been copies of the Pentateuch in the north, and it is certainly possible that the Samaritans would have had an early copy. The copy now in existence dates much later, and many scholars believe it was introduced by Manasseh at the time when the Samaritan sanctuary was established on Mount Gerizim.

The question of the origin of the Samaritan Pentateuch involves technicalities, but later history clearly shows that the Samaritans gave great credence to the first five books of the Bible, the Pentateuch.

Shechem (the modern Nablus) is the major settlement of Samaria today, there being about 200 Samaritans who observe the law and even keep the Passover on Mount Gerizim. They demonstrate remarkable exactness based on the Mosaic laws as found in their Samaritan Pentateuch.

The Samaritan Pentateuch does not date back to the times of Moses but it is an interesting reminder of the way the Pentateuch has been copied and preserved through the centuries.

The Sacred Bull

The sacred bull Apis was an important god, especially at Memphis (as pictured). At the time of the ten plagues, it was seriously discredited when the cattle were destroyed. When the Israelites constructed a golden calf, possibly Apis was in mind.

We have already referred to Memphis which would have been the major capital of Egypt in the days when Joseph was there, and later when the Hebrews were slaves. The chief god of Memphis was Ptah, supposedly the creator of the whole universe. The sacred bull Apis was believed to be a living manifestation of Ptah and later the sacred bull was combined with the god of the under-world, Osiris, to form the deity Serapis. We go a few miles across country to the extension as it were of Memphis, and we find the Serapeum at Saqqara. Not only was this a great burial place for the Pharaoh Zozer, but it was also the burial place for a large number of these sacred bulls.

In 1850, Auguste Mariett hired men and started digging at Saqqara and found some 150 sphinxes along an avenue about 600 feet long. This led to a temple and the famous Serapeum, the burial ground of the sacred bull Apis.

When the Hebrews set up a calf to worship in the wilderness, in the absence of Moses who was up on the mountain being given the laws from God, possibly they were thinking of the worship of the bull Apis that they had seen so often in Egypt.

The Serpent Motif

This serpent motif was found on an incense bowl at Beth-shean. The serpent is a well-known motif in ancient religions, worshiped not only in Egypt but in Babylonia and other areas as well. When we come to the story of the fall of man, the serpent was not merely a talking snake but was Satan himself (Rev. 12:9; 20:2), possessing and using a serpent's body to deceive Eve.

As shown in Ezekiel 28:13-15, Satan was originally created as the highest of all angels, the "anointed cherub" covering the very throne of God in heaven. He and all the angels had been created to be "ministering spirits sent forth to minister for those who will inherit salvation" (Heb. 1:14). Dr. Henry Morris is one scholar who has pointed out that Satan was not content with a role inferior in two important respects to man — angels were not created in God's image, nor could they reproduce after their kind, there being no "female" angels.

Further, Satan led one-third of the angels to rebel against God (Rev. 12:4-9), seeking to become God himself. God therefore "cast him to the earth" (Ezek. 28:17). On a temporary basis, God in His sovereignty allowed Satan to tempt the very ones he had been created to serve.

The significance given to the ancient serpent — not only in Egypt but right through the ancient world — reminds us of the way the Bible identifies the serpent as a symbol for the devil and evil idolatry. This serpent was on an incense vessel at Beth-shean.

The Serpent on a Pole

And the Lord said to Moses, Make a fiery serpent and set it upon a pole: and it shall come to pass that every one that is bitten, when he looks on it, shall live (Num. 21:8).

Although this is only one of at least 40 miracles that took place during the Exodus and wilderness wanderings, this miracle is especially important as a prophecy of the coming work of Christ on the cross. "As Moses lifted up the serpent in the wilderness," said Jesus, "even so must the Son of Man be lifted up: that whoever believes in Him should not perish, but have eternal life" (John 3:14-15).

Sin, symbolized by the serpent, must be put to death. If the sinner would live, that death must be appropriated in faith as his own deserved death. Jesus Christ was made "to be sin for us, He who knew no sin; that we might be made the righteousness of God in Him" (2 Cor. 5:21). As in the wilderness, salvation is now available to those who "look and live."

On the Top of Mount Nebo

This is Mount Nebo, some 4,000 feet above the Dead Sea. It offers a magnificent view across into Israel west of the Jordan. On a clear day it is possible to see right across to Jerusalem.

Somewhere here before he died Moses was able to see the land that his people were to possess. He was not to enter it because of his sin in striking the rock a second time, when he had been told to speak to it. Spiritually and symbolically, he spoiled the type of Christ: "that rock that followed them was Christ," the Apostle Paul said (1 Cor. 10:4). Thus, when Moses struck the rock after having been told to speak to it, he was spoiling that type. The striking of our Lord at Calvary could take place only once.

The Serpent on a Pole

This interesting stone symbol is on Mount Nebo, in the general area where Moses died. It is a reminder of the incident in the wilderness where a bronze serpent had to be put on a pole. Whoever looked would be healed from the bite of the serpent.

Moses was buried in this general area of Mount Nebo, but nobody knows where because the Scripture tells us that he was buried by God. That was not his ultimate end: we have a reminder of that when we see him alive in the presence of our Lord on the Mount of Transfiguration (Luke 9:30).

Mount Nebo

This stone memorial on the top of Mount Nebo was put there by local people, as an interesting reminder that somewhere in this area the great man Moses died. The land of Israel across the Jordan can be clearly seen (Deut. 34:1-7).

SECTION II

A GREATER-THAN-MOSES IS HERE

Moses Was a Servant but Christ Was a Son

And Moses indeed was faithful in all His house as a servant . . .
but Christ as a Son over His own house . . ." (Heb. 3:5-6).

In many ways Moses can be compared with the Lord Jesus Christ, and in such a comparison we find Christ is superior over and over again. Our Lord, like Moses, was of a priestly line, but the Lord Jesus Christ was spiritually of the priestly line of Melchizedek. We read in the Epistle to the Hebrews that He is a Priest for ever, after the order of Melchizedek. Moses was of the line of Levi, the line that was inferior to that of Melchizedek, as that same Epistle to the Hebrews makes clear. Melchizedek is a picture of Him who is eternal, having no beginning or ending, the One who ever lives to make intercession for us. The sons of Levi could act as priests only in their lifetime, but Jesus Christ ever lives and is our eternal High Priest. We elaborate on this in our section on Aaron: "A Greater-Than-Aaron Is Here."

Divine Protection

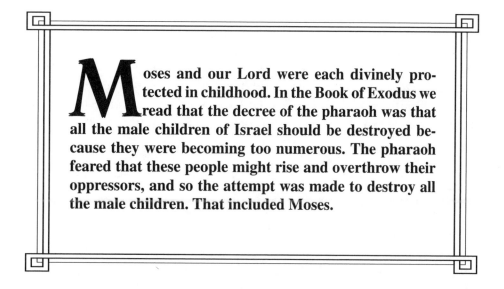

Moses and our Lord were each divinely protected in childhood. In the Book of Exodus we read that the decree of the pharaoh was that all the male children of Israel should be destroyed because they were becoming too numerous. The pharaoh feared that these people might rise and overthrow their oppressors, and so the attempt was made to destroy all the male children. That included Moses.

Similarly, when the Lord Jesus Christ was born, those Wise Men who made the mistake of coming to Jerusalem instead of to Bethlehem were the cause of the king having the ancient records searched. The Wise Men were told they must go to Bethlehem where the Christ Child would be born. Herod then set out to destroy the Child, for he feared that this One would overthrow him, and he knew that the Jewish people were looking for a Messiah who would be their King. So King Herod took steps to ensure that the Baby would be destroyed. He was not successful, of course, just as the attempt on the life of Moses was unsuccessful. A greater-than-Moses was here: this Baby born in Bethlehem was the Eternal One who had been forever in the will of the Father. No petty Herod could so much as put a finger on that Divine Child, unless it was allowed by God. Indeed, He was himself the very author of life, the One who could say, "I am the life" (John 14:6).

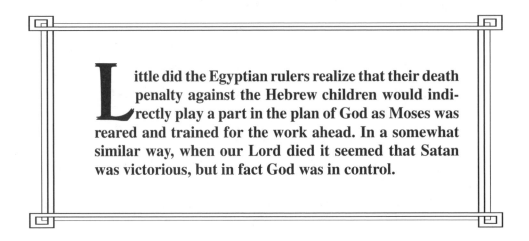

Little did the Egyptian rulers realize that their death penalty against the Hebrew children would indirectly play a part in the plan of God as Moses was reared and trained for the work ahead. In a somewhat similar way, when our Lord died it seemed that Satan was victorious, but in fact God was in control.

Another point of comparison is that Moses and our Lord were each entrusted to a man and a woman of God. Moses' parents protected him even though it meant going against the edict of a pharaoh, and their faith is recorded in that wonderful faith chapter, Hebrews 11. The same type of courage was shown by Joseph and Mary who obeyed God, both in taking our Lord into Egypt, and then in returning with Him from Egypt.

One of the Royal Family

Moses was adopted into the royal family of Egypt, and possibly he was reared as the foster-brother of the man against whom he was later to declare the judgment of God. The Lord Jesus Christ had no need to be adopted into the royal family, for He is himself the King of kings, the very Son of God. Yet though He is the Son of God He did not think it "robbery" to be equal with God (Phil. 2:6). He is himself God in flesh.

The eternal King stepped down into time and was born of the royal line of David: He was Israel's rightful King. The Son of God who was King of kings became the Son of Man, and heir to the throne of David.

The Scripture tells us that Moses was instructed in all the wisdom of the Egyptians: he had the advantage of the best education that the world of his day could offer.

We know much concerning ancient Egyptian education. These people who much earlier had been capable of building the great pyramids, which today are such a popular tourist attraction, were also capable of much that equals, and sometimes even surpasses, the understanding of many great minds today. Moses was the product of a very advanced culture and environment, and he was ideally trained of God for the important work of leading the people of Israel into nationhood.

A subject too seldom looked at today is that of the education of the Lord Jesus Christ. In the time of our Lord the education of Jewish boys was quite remarkable by ancient standards, with both primary and secondary education at a high standard. Our Lord would have had such an education — witness His teachings that involved mathematics and the knowledge of the history of His people. But our Lord did not only increase in wisdom and stature and in favor with God and man (Luke 2:52), but He was also the Son of God. As Son of Man He laid aside His glory to increase in knowledge; as God He was himself the very fount of wisdom and of knowledge. A greater-than-Moses was here.

A Greater Deliverance from a Greater Bondage

The Hebrew people were in bondage when Moses was born, but he was chosen of God to lead them out of bondage. The Lord Jesus Christ came to earth because the world itself was in bondage, not only to a pharaoh but to the forces of evil who had set themselves up against the living God. Christ came to oppose and destroy the power of the spiritual enemy, and He did so victoriously.

We have seen that Moses was trained in all the wisdom of the Egyptians, and then he learned much about God in a long wilderness experience. The Lord Jesus Christ had been "the darling of His Father's bosom" through eternity, but the time came when He, too, went into a wilderness experience. The heavens had opened as God declared, "This is My Beloved Son, in whom I am well pleased," yet not long afterwards the heavens were dark as this One was forsaken of God. This was an experience Moses never knew, for only the Lord Jesus could be forsaken in this way as He who knew no sin became sin for us.

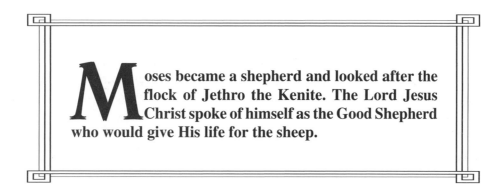

Moses became a shepherd and looked after the flock of Jethro the Kenite. The Lord Jesus Christ spoke of himself as the Good Shepherd who would give His life for the sheep.

After many long years as a shepherd, God led Moses out into a lonely part of the wilderness, to the experience of a burning bush that was not consumed. At that time Moses was told that God had chosen him to redeem the Israelites from slavery.

The Great I Am

Moses hesitated to go against the pharaoh, and he asked such questions as, "Whom shall I say has sent me?" This was when God revealed Himself as the great I Am — the ever-living One, the Almighty God. This is implied in that title, "I Am that I Am," as we have already seen in chapter 3.

In John's Gospel we read many times of the Lord Jesus Christ referring to himself as "I Am." He used an emphatic form in the Greek as He declared *ego eimi*, "I, even I, Am." He did not only say *eimi*, "I Am," but *ego eimi*, "I, even I, Am." The Lord Jesus Christ could say, "I Am the bread of God," "I Am the way," "I Am the truth," "I Am the life," "I Am the Resurrection," "I Am — the Messiah." This One who claimed to be God also demonstrated His deity by signs such as the raising of Lazarus from the dead. A greater-than-Moses is here, even the One who lives today, the ever-great and living I Am — the Son of God himself.

We have said that Moses hesitated to go against the pharaoh, and he asked such questions as, "What shall I say?" He argued that he was not an eloquent man, and he asked for someone such as his brother Aaron to go with him. How different is the Lord Jesus Christ who could say, "Here am I, send Me." He could always declare, "I delight to do My Father's will."

The prophecy of Isaiah tells us much about the Son of God who was the divine servant, the One chosen of Jehovah, and as we examine the records of His life we find that He was ever the willing servant. Philippians 2 reminds us that He was even obedient unto death, the death of the cross.

Moses was a man meek above all men on the earth. The Lord Jesus Christ said of himself, "Take My yoke upon you and learn from Me, for I am gentle and lowly in heart" (Matt. 11:29). He was the King of kings, yet He came riding on a donkey into Jerusalem. A greater-than-Moses was here, for this One Who was so meek and lowly in heart was also the Creator of all those for whom He displayed that wonderful meekness.

Moses was obviously a man of some failings, but he was possessed of great potential, for God had specially chosen him to be His servant. Though sometimes reluctant, Moses proved by his life that he was indeed dedicated to the Lord and to His people.

Contending with Masters of Evil

Both Moses and our Lord contended with masters of evil. Moses went against the pharaoh who was the representative of the evil forces in opposition to God, but Jesus Christ went against the very personification of evil forces when He went out into the wilderness and was tested by the devil. Satan offered the Lord all the kingdoms of the earth if Jesus would but fall down and worship Satan himself. Each time Jesus was tempted He came back to the Word of God as He declared: "It is written. . . . It is written. . . . It is written. . . ."

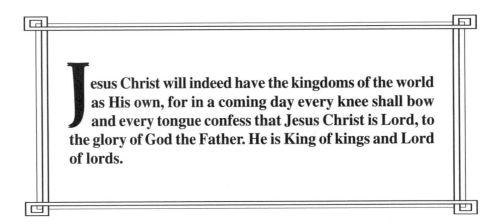

Jesus Christ will indeed have the kingdoms of the world as His own, for in a coming day every knee shall bow and every tongue confess that Jesus Christ is Lord, to the glory of God the Father. He is King of kings and Lord of lords.

Moses was but the representative of his people: he was as a servant in the house of God, but Jesus Christ was the Son in the house (Heb. 3:5-6). Moses was the representative of the Heavenly King, but Jesus Christ is himself the King of kings.

After the conflict with pharaoh, involving the ten plagues by which it was shown that the gods of Egypt were powerless, Moses led the children of Israel out of bondage. Jesus Christ in a far greater way showed how powerless the opposing gods were, for He cast out evil spirits. By His ultimate victory over death He destroyed the power of him who had the power of death. Today He continues to set the captive free, for as He himself said, "If the Son makes you free, you shall be free indeed" (John 8:36). A greater-than-Moses is here. . . . One who is worthy of more glory than Moses (Heb. 3:3).

There are many other points of comparison between Moses and our Lord. Each spoke as the prophet of God. On his part, Moses looked ahead to the Lord Jesus Christ when in Deuteronomy 18 he said that God would raise up unto His people a prophet like unto Moses himself. In the fullness of time our Lord came as a prophet to His people, yet this One who came was not just a prophet as Moses was: He was the *Logos*, the Word of God, the very manifestation of the wisdom of God. Because of this the Christian can now say, "Christ who became for us wisdom" (1 Cor. 1:30). A greater-than-Moses is here, One who could even say, "I and My Father are One" (John 10:30).

Moses was but a voice, whereas Jesus was the Word. Moses was a pupil in the school of God, but Jesus was himself the Master Teacher. Moses feared when he came into the revealed presence of God (Exod. 3:6), whereas our Lord ever sought the intimate presence of God, and would spend nights alone in prayer.

The Passover Is Celebrated

When the Exodus from Egypt was about to take place, Moses was instructed by the Lord to tell the Israelites that each household should take a lamb, shed its blood, and apply it to the doors of their homes. When the destroying angel saw the blood he would pass over and all those in the house would be safe. This is known as the Passover, when the destroying angel did "pass over," and those inside the houses were safe, just as the Lord had said. When we go to the first letter of the apostle Paul to the Corinthian Christians we read, "Christ our Passover was sacrificed for us" (1 Cor. 5:7).

Those Israelites year by year celebrated the annual feast of the Passover; it was the time when they especially remembered the Lord's great deliverance of His people from Egypt. Christians look back to Calvary when the Lamb of God offered HIMSELF to bear away our sins, and we recognize that a greater Passover has been sacrificed for us — the Lamb of God himself.

Ours is a greater deliverance from a greater bondage, even the bondage of spiritual death. Moses could but take a lamb as a symbol, pointing on to the Lamb of God, for Christ himself was the Lamb. The Good Shepherd became the Lamb who would give His life for the sheep. A greater-than-Moses is here.

By the Passover we are also reminded that both Moses and our Lord established memorials. We have seen that Moses established the celebration of the Passover which looked forward to Jesus Christ who was the fulfillment of that memorial. Jesus also established a memorial when He instituted the memorial supper, the remembrance feast of the bread and the wine, speaking of His body broken and His blood shed for our redemption.

Both Moses and the Lord Jesus Christ established covenants: Moses instituted the old covenant of the Law, but Jesus came to give that new covenant of which Jeremiah spoke, the new covenant to be sealed by the death of the One making the covenant. It was sealed in His own blood, and so He said, "This is the NEW Covenant in My blood" (Luke 22:20).

Both Moses and our Lord controlled the sea — Moses when he led the children of Israel to a new freedom, across the Red Sea which opened when he raised his rod; and the Lord Jesus Christ from a boat when He rebuked the troubled storm and said, "Peace, be still!" This One was the Master of the tempest and of all the elements, for by Him all things are held together (Col. 1:17).

Bread from Heaven

Both Moses and our Lord fed multitudes — Moses when he was used of God to provide the manna for all those long years of the wilderness journey, manifesting the constant provision of God. But, as Christ himself reminded the Jewish leaders, Moses fed his people only for a passing time. Our Lord was himself the Living Bread of God sent down from heaven. Jesus Christ continues to feed multitudes with spiritual bread, for He is still the Bread of God, able to satisfy us spiritually as we partake of Him. Moses' ability to feed the multitudes left him at death, but the Lord Jesus Christ feeds us in His resurrection life.

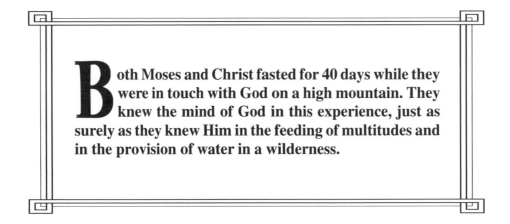

Both Moses and Christ fasted for 40 days while they were in touch with God on a high mountain. They knew the mind of God in this experience, just as surely as they knew Him in the feeding of multitudes and in the provision of water in a wilderness.

Moses was the greatest law-giver of ancient times, even greater than Hammurabi of Babylon. His code of laws can be compared with others at certain points, and this is to be expected. Where there are common experiences and environments, there are likely to be common laws. But when we consider moral and ethical values, the world has never seen a greater systematic code of laws than that which Moses gave.

Our Lord Put Himself Above Moses

Matthew 5:17-48 shows clearly that the Lord put himself above Moses. Moses had given the law as to the penalty for actual killing, but Jesus went beyond killing to the root motive of anger without a cause; Moses condemned adultery, but Jesus went on to show that even when a man looked on a woman with lust, he had already committed adultery with her in his heart. Moses condemned certain oaths, but Christ went on to the ideal where one's own word should be sufficient, without the necessity for the too-lightly-given oaths so common in His time in Palestine.

It is relevant to point out that Moses himself was in need of law, and he dealt with a people in need of law. But the Lord Jesus Christ himself was able to announce the ideal, and to demonstrate both in word and in life the ideal of God to all people everywhere. A greater-than-Moses was here. Moses was a law-giver; Jesus demonstrated the ideal to which the law pointed.

Another interesting point is where Moses says, "An eye for an eye and a tooth for a tooth." That was a wonderful provision, because in other law codes before Moses' day there was not equal restitution, as an eye for an eye implied. More likely it would have been ten eyes for an eye if the one who had been injured was a member of the nobility. But with the law of Moses it was equality — only one eye for one eye, and a tooth for a tooth. It was one for one, teaching the equality of men.

Even in this our Lord went beyond Moses' ideal of equal justice, for He urged men to love one another, to turn the other cheek, to be prepared to "go the second mile." Moses had taught his people to love each other, but they hated their enemies. Jesus came and said, "Love your enemies, bless those who curse you, pray for those who spitefully use you" (Matt. 5:44).

A greater-than-Moses was here, even the Son of God who came and offered peace and reconciliation with God for all men, everywhere, provided they came to the Father by Him. He himself was the Prince of Peace who made peace by the blood of His cross.

In the Bible Moses speaks to us of the law, and Scriptures such as Romans 5 teach that there was a curse associated with the law — the penalty of death against those who sinned. However, the Scripture also says, "For the law was given through Moses, but grace and truth came through Jesus Christ" (John 1:17).

"He Knew No Sin"

Moses himself, because of a particular act of disobedience, became ineligible to lead the people into the land. But a greater-than-Moses has come, and even His enemies could find no fault with Him. The Lord Jesus Christ could say, "Which of you convicts Me of sin?" and no man could point the finger and say, "Here, at this point, this Man has sinned."

The apostle Peter who was so intimate with Him was able to say, "He committed no sin, nor was guile found in His mouth" (1 Pet. 2:22). Those who live with people soon know some of their faults, but those who lived with the Lord Jesus Christ united to testify that this Man was sinless. A greater-than-Moses is here, for there can be no point of criticism found in the blameless and holy life of our Lord.

Moses could not give the children of Israel entrance into the Promised Land because of his own sin, but Jesus Christ was the perfect One and the captain of our salvation. Because of His own preparedness to take the sins of the people upon himself, He can give us entrance into the heavenly Promised Land. He gives the true rest for which man has been searching, and we come into the experience of peace with God even while we are on earth.

We enjoy that experience as we come to Calvary and see that the Lord Jesus Christ has borne our sins in His own body on the Cross. He took the curse of the law on himself. We bless God because though "the law was given through Moses . . . grace and truth came through Jesus Christ." A greater-than-Moses is here.

Seventy Helpers

Moses and our Lord each used 70 helpers in their great work, but a greater-than-Moses is here, for our Lord appeared after death to commission others beside the 70, to send them forth with a continuing message. That message is still the same, for as His messengers go out into the world they urge men to live for Him who died for them.

Both Moses and the Lord Jesus Christ offered great prayers for their people — Moses was even prepared to be shut off from the presence of God rather than have his people forsaken. The Lord Jesus Christ was in fact shut off from the presence of God when He was forsaken on the Cross. We hear Him cry,

"My God, why hast thou forsaken Me?" and we know the answer: there was no other way in which salvation could be made available to us. A greater-than-Moses was here, for by offering himself He could deliver even the enemies of God.

Even if Moses had been cut off from the people this would not have led to their salvation, for Moses was but a man. But the Son of God could offer himself, and because He is infinite He could bear the penalty of the sins of the whole world.

Re-appearance After Death

Both Moses and the Lord Jesus Christ reappeared after death, for this is part of the great teaching of Scripture. Moses reminds us that there is life beyond the grave. He assures us that there is not just soul-sleep for those who pass on, but he encourages us to believe the great hope of the Christian — that we shall be glorified with Jesus Christ. We see Moses on the Mount of Transfiguration, alive, in the presence of his Lord.

Those who have lost loved ones who knew the Lord need not sorrow as those without hope: loved ones who have died "in the Lord" are in His presence. As the apostle Paul reminds us, they are absent from the body, present with the Lord.

Moses was but a man, and of course he was dependent on God for his life to continue. But the Lord Jesus Christ said of himself, "I lay down My life that I might take it again" (John 10:17). "No man takes it from Me," He said, "I lay it down of myself . . . to take it again." He was himself the very source of life, and yet, in the mystery of the redemption that was available only through himself, He laid down His life voluntarily.

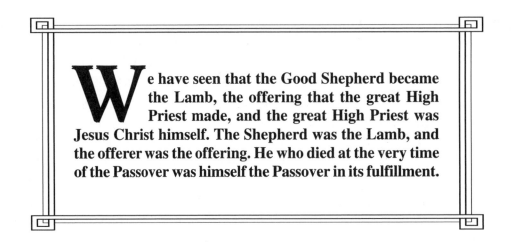

We have seen that the Good Shepherd became the Lamb, the offering that the great High Priest made, and the great High Priest was Jesus Christ himself. The Shepherd was the Lamb, and the offerer was the offering. He who died at the very time of the Passover was himself the Passover in its fulfillment.

Jesus took up His life again after death, and He lives today. He is alive, seated in the presence of the Father on high, promising eternal life to all those who will walk with Him. A greater-than-Moses is here, for in the power of Christ's resurrection life we, too, can look beyond the grave to new life in the presence of God forever. Christ is "the first-fruits" — and we shall share that same resurrection life.

All this is made possible because of the fulfillment of Moses' own prediction. The Lord did raise up "a Prophet like me from your midst, from your brethren" (Deut. 18:15). Our Lord became flesh, taking upon himself the nature of a man so that as a man He could die. Only as a man could He die for our sins, and so He came as a prophet, one of His own people. He came to die, and because He died, we live. Because He became like His brethren, we have become His brethren whom He presents before His Father

(Heb. 2:11-13, 17). What a privileged position is ours!

Moses was a faithful servant in God's house. We who know Christ have become sons of God (John 1:12); we are heirs of God, and joint-heirs with Christ (Rom. 8:17). A greater-than-Moses is here, even He who has redeemed us by His blood.

Jesus Was Worthy of More Glory Than Moses

Christ Jesus . . . has been counted worthy of
more glory than Moses (Heb. 3:1-3).

"He dwelt among us, and we
beheld His glory" (John 1:14).

Moses was called onto the Mount with God and there he saw something of the outshining of the glory of the Lord. When he came back to the people he had to put a veil on, because the glory of God could be seen in his face. Even on the mountain itself Moses had to be covered in that first experience of the glory of God passing by. In symbolism it was made clear that there were some things not available to him. But through faith in Jesus Christ, Christians can have a fuller view of the glory of God, and we are told we can behold His glory. We have seen something of the spiritual outshining of the glory of God in the face of Jesus Christ.

Glory on a Mountain

Thinking of glory reminds us of another aspect of the superiority of Jesus Christ to Moses, displayed on that day when our Lord took the three intimate disciples, Peter, James, and John, onto a mountain. There He was transfigured — "metamorphosed" is the literal word. This word actually means that He was changed, as though into another being. When a beautiful butterfly bursts forth from a cocoon there is a metamorphosis — we cannot recognize the beautiful creature that is now flying against the sunlight as the rather ugly cocoon from which it emerged. There has been a metamorphosis.

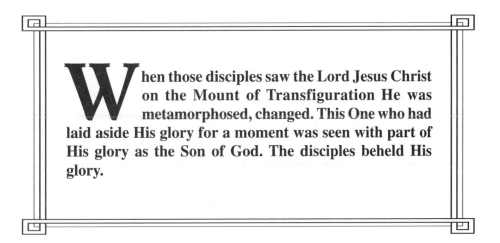

When those disciples saw the Lord Jesus Christ on the Mount of Transfiguration He was metamorphosed, changed. This One who had laid aside His glory for a moment was seen with part of His glory as the Son of God. The disciples beheld His glory.

We have referred to our Lord's appearance on the Mount of Transfiguration with Moses and Elijah. On that Mount it was the exodus, or departure, of the Lord Jesus Christ which Moses and Elijah talked about, and not the exodus of their own experience. Moses led a wonderful exodus from Egypt, and Elijah's personal exodus was spectacular, for he was translated into the presence of God. But a greater-than-Moses-and-Elijah, was there on the Mount of Transfiguration, even the Son of God himself.

Though the disciples were afraid, they were yet able to behold His glory. In the prayer of Jesus Christ in John 17, that great prayer of intercession, we hear Him say, "Father, I desire that they also whom You gave Me may be with Me where I am, that they may behold My glory." Jesus Christ wants us, like those disciples, to be in a mountaintop experience with himself, beholding His glory.

Moses saw a little of the glory of God, and the children of Israel saw it reflected on his face. The Lord Jesus Christ was himself God. It was His own glory which He manifested there on the Mount of Trans-figuration, and not just a reflected glory such as the children of Israel saw in Moses . . . yet He laid aside His glory and went into the darkness of death so that He could bring US to himself. Surely a greater-than-Moses is here.

Sufferings . . . and the Glories That Would Follow

Let us summarize some aspects that touch the glory of Christ. In 1 Peter 1:11 we read of the suffer-ings of Christ and the glories that would follow. Our Lord suffered, but afterwards He was glorified and sat at the right hand of the Majesty on high.

Moses was rejected by his brethren, as was our Lord. When Moses first sided with his own people he found that he was the object of criticism and was forced to flee because of the possible consequences of having killed an Egyptian who was oppressing one of the Hebrew slaves. There were other times when Moses was rejected, especially in the wilderness when numbers of his own people suggested that they should return to Egypt where there was a greater variety of foodstuffs than in the wilderness.

We have read in John 1:11 that our Lord Jesus Christ came unto His own and His own did not receive Him. We are also told that even His brethren did not believe in Him (John 7:5). We are not surprised, for when we go again to the prophecy of Isaiah we learn that this One was to be despised and rejected of men.

While he was in rejection Moses took to himself a bride from outside his own people, for he married one of the daughters of Jethro the Kenite. Again we see the similarity to the life of our Lord: His own people rejected Him but now He has taken to himself a bride, for His Church is described as the bride of Christ, made up of Jew and Gentile alike. One of the longest descriptions in the Revelation, the last book of the Bible, is of the bride of Christ. She is shown in her glory, reminding us of our Lord's prayer in John 17 where He said, "The glory which you gave Me I have given them."

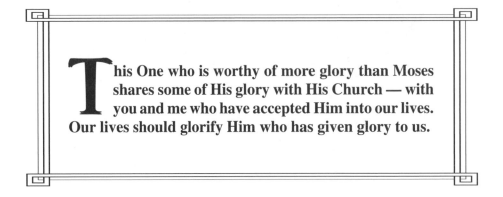

This One who is worthy of more glory than Moses shares some of His glory with His Church — with you and me who have accepted Him into our lives. Our lives should glorify Him who has given glory to us.

The Tabernacle Displayed His Glory

In the wilderness Moses was able to give the people a tabernacle which spoke of the presence of God. That tabernacle could not be given until they were out in the wilderness journey, and there is a perfect illustration here of spiritual principles. The children of Israel could not know the presence of God in this visible sense until they were redeemed. God is ever seeking those who would worship Him, but the visible symbol of the presence of God could not be known to the people of Israel until they had come out of the land of Egypt and its bondage. So after they had crossed through the Red Sea Moses told them to build a tabernacle for God, a place where God would dwell.

In a fuller sense we today know this privilege, too, for after His death on Calvary where the Lord Jesus Christ delivered us from the bondage of Satan, it became possible for us to know the presence of God. We come to Calvary and we see the great deliverance available to us, and we understand that we can know practical deliverance from the powers of sin and of evil. So we worship, and we are enabled to practice the presence of Christ.

This then is one of the great lessons we learn from that tabernacle in the wilderness. They were in a wilderness, but God would be with them. Today we are in a wilderness journey, for, as Peter the Apostle reminds us, we are pilgrims and strangers on the earth. But though we are pilgrims and strangers, the Lord Jesus Christ has said, "I am with you always, even to the end of the age."

There is a spiritual parallel here for us. Moses was able to tell these people of a tabernacle, and he gave them all the details as to how that tabernacle was to be erected, and the Lord said through Moses that he must construct it according to the given pattern (Exod. 25:9, 40). So it is with us today. We, too, are on a pilgrimage journey, but God has been pleased to come down and dwell with us.

As we read at the beginning of John's Gospel, the Lord Jesus Christ himself has "tabernacled" amongst us, and has shown us His glory. His home is in heaven, but He "camped out" for a while, for our redemption.

Temples of the Living God

Today it is our privilege to go forth to Jesus Christ outside the camp, bearing His reproach — just as Hebrews 11 tells us Moses did, and yet in that wilderness journey God is with us. Yes, a greater-than-Moses is here. Moses could only erect a tabernacle which would speak of God, but Jesus Christ himself came and tabernacled amongst men. Now those who are believers in Him, those who are His disciples, are indwelt by the Spirit of God. The apostle Paul tells us that we have become temples of the living God. We are those in whom God would dwell and manifest forth His glory, and make it possible for men to know that God is indeed dwelling with men.

The time came when the Light of the World said to His disciples, "You are the lights of the world," and now those who are Christians shine forth as lights in a dark place. A greater-than-Moses is here, for the glory of God in Jesus Christ is seen in the faces of those who are truly His followers. These have become the temple of God.

Let us go on through the centuries, on to New Testament times, and watch as the apostle Paul goes to a place called Mars Hill and there reasons with the people of Athens. "God does not dwell in temples made with hands," he told them in Acts 17. Paul was in an area of many temples, for this was the center of speculation as to the various philosophies and ideas about the gods. The magnificent Parthenon held pride of place, but all around him there were temples, and we can imagine him pointing to them as he declared, "God does not dwell in temples made with hands."

That same Apostle was the one who revealed to the Christian Church that God would dwell with men in their individual lives. He also taught them that God would dwell in the midst of His Church as a body, but we are thinking here especially that God would dwell with men as individuals. No longer is God unknown — despite those men in Athens who worshiped many gods, including the "Unknown God." God had made himself known in the person of Jesus Christ, His own Son.

Showing Forth the Glory of God

This is the principle that Moses was showing the people as they came out of bondage, as they were delivered, as they went into that wilderness journey and began to build the tabernacle which would show forth the glory of God. In many ways the tabernacle pointed on to the Lord Jesus Christ, for it included such things as Aaron's rod that budded, and some of the manna, both of which were symbols of Christ. The new life on Aaron's rod pointed to the new life in Christ, and the manna spoke of Christ the living Bread, ever able to sustain us on our spiritual pilgrimage. As the tabernacle spoke of God's glory, so too we who are God's temple today should just as surely show forth the glory of God before men.

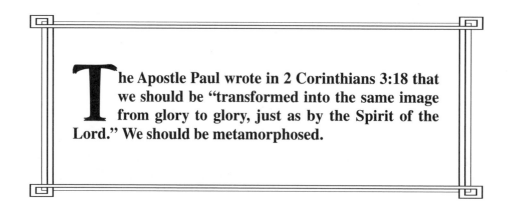

The Apostle Paul wrote in 2 Corinthians 3:18 that we should be "transformed into the same image from glory to glory, just as by the Spirit of the Lord." We should be metamorphosed.

We shall consider a few more spiritual applications from the life of Moses, God's chosen deliverer.

That Spiritual Rock Was Christ

They all drank the same spiritual drink: for they drank of that spiritual Rock that followed them, and that Rock was Christ (1 Cor. 10:4).

In this verse it is made clear that there were spiritual lessons from these factual experiences for these people in their wilderness journey. It tells us, "That Rock that followed them was Christ." In the wilderness the people needed water, so God told Moses to strike a certain rock — and from it flowed beautiful clear water.

In passing it is interesting to mention that Jewish people today point to a particular rock which they identify as the rock that Moses struck. We cannot of course insist that this was the actual rock, though the tradition is by no means a new one.

We go on, and we read of Moses striking the rock a second time when on this occasion he had been told to SPEAK to it (Num. 20:7-12). By striking it this second time he was spoiling the type, for as our verse reminds us, "That Rock which followed them was Christ." The Rock Christ was to be struck only once at Calvary, and so Moses was spoiling the type. As a result he could not lead his people into the Promised Land — but he did appear, alive, on the Mount of Transfiguration!

Living Water

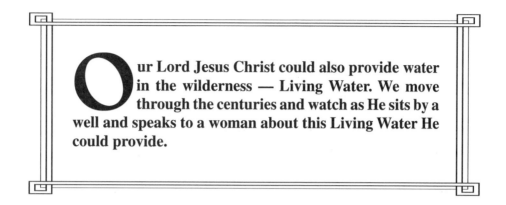

Our Lord Jesus Christ could also provide water in the wilderness — Living Water. We move through the centuries and watch as He sits by a well and speaks to a woman about this Living Water He could provide.

In John 4 we learn that the Samaritan woman wanted this Living Water so that she would not need to come and draw water day by day. Instead Jesus was speaking of himself as One who could give Living Water, freely provided to those who would come to Him. He was referring to the water of the Spirit of God, Water which could cause a man's life to be as a river overflowing with joy and satisfaction even though he was a pilgrim and a stranger in a barren wilderness. As Moses provided the people with water in the wilderness, it was a spiritual lesson pointing to Christ.

Similarly in Exodus 15 there is another spiritual lesson from an interesting story of a tree being cast into bitter waters, and the waters becoming sweet. Here we have a figure of Calvary. The waters were unsatisfying, disappointing, but the tree of Calvary has been cast into the waters of despair and disappointment, and they have become sweet. As our Lord said to that Samaritan woman, whoever comes to Him will know rivers of living water flowing from his innermost being. Moses could provide water that would satisfy temporarily. Jesus gave spiritual water, — not just for our wilderness journey, but eternally satisfying.

Life for a Look

Christ himself endorsed this approach of presenting spiritual truths from the events of the Exodus and the wilderness journey.

One incident was when the children of Israel had complained so much against God and His provision for them that He sent fiery serpents among them. When they repented, Moses was told to make a serpent of bronze and to put it on a pole, and whoever looked at it was healed. There was no healing through medicines or self-treatment: the only way to be healed was to look and live.

In the New Testament story about Nicodemus, who came to the Lord by night, this incident is referred to. In the Greek, Nicodemus is referred to as "THE ruler of the Jews" (John 3:1). If all the answers had been given by Moses surely THIS man would have known them. But no! So one night Nicodemus sought Jesus in the quietness. Nicodemus wanted to know the great truths of the kingdom of God. Jesus said, "You must be born again!" As He explained the new birth He took this illustration of the children of

Israel out in the wilderness, and said, "As Moses lifted up the serpent in the wilderness, even so must the Son of Man be lifted up."

The Lord Jesus Christ himself was to become sin for us. That serpent lifted up on a pole in the wilderness spoke of sin, for the serpent in the Scriptures is the symbol of sin, and Jesus Christ himself became a curse for us when He who knew no sin became sin for us. He paid the penalty imposed by God in the law of Moses. He took the judgment of sin upon himself, and today there is salvation and healing to all those who will "look and live." As the hymn says,

> There is life for a look at the crucified One,
> There is life at this moment for thee.
> Then look, sinner, look unto Him and be saved —
> Unto Him Who was nailed to the tree;
> Look, look, look and live."

Thus we see that in the incident of the serpent in the wilderness, there is again a pointing to the Lord Jesus Christ. Moses himself could not save those people in all their distress. He could merely obey the voice of God and lift up the serpent on the pole, to provide salvation for all who looked. There was no point in anybody binding up the wounds of someone else, for salvation and healing could not be known in that way. It is not enough today to go about doing good to others, binding up their wounds as it were, for salvation is available only by looking to the Lord Jesus Christ on the cross.

As we again read that discussion with the Jewish ruler Nicodemus we realize afresh that a greater-than-Moses is here. Jesus Christ who was himself lifted up is the One whose healing power is available through the centuries, across the climates and the cultures, for whosoever will may come. Whosoever will may look and live.

It is also true that those who refuse to look can only know the judgment of God on their sin. This is made clear in the incident of the serpent in the wilderness, and it is also emphasized in the teachings of Christ. Both Moses and Christ did not hesitate to pronounce judgment against those who rejected their message as the revelation of God. Again we see the superiority of our Lord, because we read in John 5:22, "The Father judges no man, but has committed all judgment to the Son." He is the judge of all men, but it is wonderful to realize that this One who is the judge is also the deliverer of all those who will accept the penalty which He has himself paid by His death.

The Offerings Pointed to Christ

Yet another way in which Moses gave typical teaching concerning Christ was in the various offerings which he instructed the Israelites to keep. At the same time that the law was given, we find instructions given regarding a whole series of offerings, and all these pointed to Christ. He is our meal offering, the One whose perfect character was displayed before men. He was the only One who could always say, "I have glorified You on the earth." He is our burnt offering, the One whose life was wholly given to God in service: His whole life was offered as a living sacrifice before God.

For the Christian there is a practical application of this principle as seen in Romans 12:1-2. There the apostle Paul urges the Christian to present his body a living sacrifice, holy, acceptable to God, as his reasonable service. Following Christ involves more than the preparedness to die for Him: it involves preparedness to live for Him. Many a saint has found it harder to LIVE for his Lord than to DIE for Him.

Christ Is Our Peace Offering

He is our peace offering: He made peace by the offering of himself, and He now says, "My peace I give you." He himself is our sin offering, the One who took our sin upon himself.

He is our trespass offering, and we are reminded of His washing of His disciples' feet: "He who is bathed needs only to wash his feet, but is completely clean" (John 13:10). Once our sins have been washed away, as it were, at Calvary, we are saved. We are born again. Still we need to confess our sins, and He is faithful and just to forgive us our sins, and to cleanse us from all unrighteousness (1 John 1:9). Our spiritual bodies have been washed once and for all at Calvary, but our feet need to have the dust of the road washed off as a daily experience. In this way Christ is our trespass offering, ever able to give forgiveness and cleansing of our failings as mortals. Thank God, He knows our frame, that we are but dust, and forgiveness is constantly available.

In these ways Scripture assures us that it is possible for us to enjoy the Lord Jesus Christ in practical experience.

Beginning at Moses

As we conclude, we watch two early disciples walking sadly along the road to a village called Emmaus. Christ had been crucified, and their hopes had been dashed. They had thought He would be Israel's Redeemer, but the chief priests and rulers of the Jews delivered Him to death by crucifixion. Suddenly a third one caught up to them on the road and began to walk with them. "What kind of conversation is this that you have with one another as you walk and are sad?" He asked.

"Are you the only stranger in Jerusalem, and have You not known the things which happened there in these days?" asked Cleopas, not knowing that he was talking to the risen Christ. He went on to explain that Jesus of Nazareth had been a prophet, mighty in deed and word before God and all the people, and he told of how their hopes had been dashed when this One had been crucified. So the conversation went on until at last the risen Christ said:

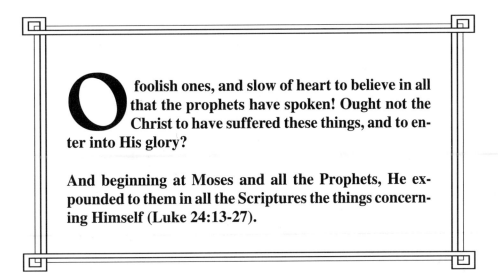

O foolish ones, and slow of heart to believe in all that the prophets have spoken! Ought not the Christ to have suffered these things, and to enter into His glory?

And beginning at Moses and all the Prophets, He expounded to them in all the Scriptures the things concerning Himself (Luke 24:13-27).

What a wonderful discourse it must have been! Little wonder that later as they talked about it they said, "Did not our heart burn within us while He talked with us on the road, and while He opened the Scriptures to us?" (Luke 24:32).

May we — you and I — continue to know the experience of the burning heart as we walk with Him — not to Emmaus, but to Jerusalem and Judea and Samaria and to the uttermost parts of the earth (Acts 1:8).

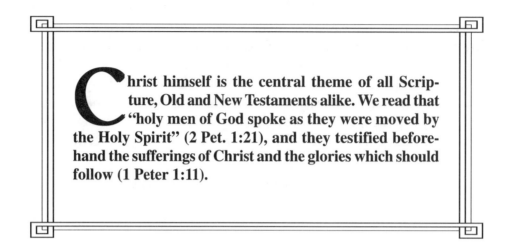

Christ himself is the central theme of all Scripture, Old and New Testaments alike. We read that "holy men of God spoke as they were moved by the Holy Spirit" (2 Pet. 1:21), and they testified beforehand the sufferings of Christ and the glories which should follow (1 Peter 1:11).

So the disciples knew the experience of the burning heart. The Scripture tells us that Jesus Christ is the same yesterday and today and forever, and He continues to walk on the road to Emmaus . . . to San Francisco . . . to Melbourne . . . to London . . . to Singapore . . . yes, and to Peking. This prophet like unto Moses still challenges men and women, and boys and girls, as He invites them to "Come, follow Me!"

As we follow, we find that the spiritual rock in the wilderness is still the Christ, able to satisfy us with Living Water, even the Water of the Spirit of God himself.

Dramatic Support for Moses, the Writer

As we bring this section to a close, it is relevant to comment on an important discovery that dramatically highlights the integrity of the law of Moses. It is a unity, and it dates to the middle of the second millennium B.C.

This destroys the infamous Documentary Hypothesis which argues that the writing of the Pentateuch stretched over many centuries, up to the time of Ezra. This has been exploded by the Hittite Covenant Treaties about which Professor George Mendenhall of Michigan has written so convincingly.

The Pattern of Hittite Covenants

Professor Mendenhall has demonstrated that covenants dating to the second half of the second millennium B.C. show a remarkable consistency, along the following lines:

1. There is a Preamble or Title, in which the author of the Covenant is identified;

2. This is followed by a Historical Prologue, outlining previous relationships between the parties concerned;

3. Detailed Stipulations which outline the obligations that the sovereign imposes on his vassal;

4. The Deposit of a copy in the sanctuary of the vassal, with regular public readings so that

the people are reminded of the terms of the Covenant;

5. The Witnesses who are invoked are actually recognized gods;

6. Curses and Blessings are listed, to be invoked according to whether the Covenant is broken or kept by the vassal.[9]

Professor Kitchen Endorses Mendenhall's Conclusions

Most covenants of the 14th/13th centuries B.C. followed this pattern closely, and usually there was also an oath of obedience, a solemn ceremony, and a statement about the formal procedure to be followed if it was necessary to take action against a rebellious vassal.

Professor Kenneth Kitchen follows Mendenhall's outline and shows that these forms are adapted to the Hebrew culture — e.g., memorial stones are placed as continuing witnesses instead of pagan gods. Dr. Kitchen analyzes the Sinai Covenant and its renewal in Exodus, Leviticus, Deuteronomy, and Joshua. He states that if these patterns are compared with known late second and first millennium treaties, "it is strikingly evident that the Sinai Covenant and its renewal must be classed with the late second millennium covenants."[10]

The covenant itself is in Exodus, chapters 20 to 31; then, after an idolatrous interlude by which the covenant was broken, it was renewed, as shown at Exodus 34. It was renewed with the new generation after the wilderness journey (Deut. 1 to 32). Joshua again presented it in Joshua 24.

We said that Professor Kitchen discusses the implications of all this to the writing of the covenant documents in Exodus, Leviticus, Deuteronomy and Joshua. Having analyzed the covenant forms in the second millennium (when compared with the first millennium), he shows that "there are clear and undeniable differences," both as to form and content. The Documentary Hypothesis simply does not make sense in light of this material.

The Whole Text Was a Unity!

If the documents were not committed to writing until the ninth to sixth centuries B.C. and beyond (as argued by the Documentary Hypothesis), it is strange that writers or redactors could so easily reproduce a biblical covenant form that had fallen out of customary usage some 300 to 600 years earlier.

Professor Kitchen goes on to show that this is tangible evidence "that considerable portions of these books" originated in the times of Moses and Joshua. Professor Kitchen makes the further point that it is not the so-called "J" or "E" version that corresponds with other Near Eastern treaty documents, "but the full, unitary text of passages such as Genesis chapter 31, Exodus 19:20, and Joshua chapter 24."[11]

This sort of objective data is yet another indication that the unsatisfactory and unsubstantiated Documentary Hypothesis should be put to one side. It does not offer a satisfactory solution to the origin of the Old Testament documents. The facts suggest that those records were basically eyewitness documents, not embellished "campfire" stories, nor were they first put into writing hundreds of years after the events described.

Talking with Professor G. Ernest Wright

Clifford Wilson adds a personal note about the relevance of the Hittite Suzerainty Treaties to the writing of Moses in the Pentateuch:

In 1969 I was an area supervisor at the excavation of Gezer in Israel. Professor G. Ernest Wright of Harvard was with us as the titular head of the prestigious American Schools of Oriental Research. One Saturday morning he gave an outstanding address to the 120-plus American college students who made up the bulk of our work force. He elaborated on the important work of Professor George Mendenhall on the Hittite Covenant documents.

Professor Wright showed the relevance of those Hittite treaties to the legal forms in the covenant documents of Moses in the Pentateuch, and he (Professor Wright) concluded that Mendenhall's researches had demonstrated two major points:

> 1. The covenant documents in the Pentateuch (the first five books of the Bible) were a unity; and
> 2. They dated to the middle of the second millennium B.C. — the time of Moses.

Those two conclusions are devastating to the Documentary Hypothesis. If the writings were a "unity," they could not be explained as different documents brought together over centuries.

Secondly, if they dated to the middle of the second millennium B.C., that was the time of Moses and not of writers AFTER the time of Solomon.

I went to Dr. Wright afterwards and respectfully said to him, "Sir, this is very different from what you have in some of your writings."

He looked at me very seriously and then he said: "Clifford, for 30 years I have been teaching students training for the Christian ministry in various institutions, including Harvard. I have told them that they can forget Moses in the Pentateuch but now, at least in these significant areas, I've had to admit that I was wrong."

Professor Wright was Professor of Semitics and Old Testament Studies at Harvard for 17 years, and was previously at other prestigious institutions. As such, he was recognized as one of the world's leading scholars in his field. And that leading scholar was literally discarding basic aspects of the outmoded Documentary Hypothesis.

It is fair to ask if the Documentary Hypothesis would have retained any credibility if it was related to any other book than the Bible. That Book has withstood hammering blows through the centuries, and the unsubstantiated blows of the Documentary Hypothesis have possibly rung the loudest, if only because of the hollowness of its arguments.

"Manifest Absurdities"

Hebrew literature grew up in the same context as other ancient Oriental literature. Professor Kitchen makes a further point that "any attempt to apply the criteria of the documentary theorists to ancient Oriental compositions that have known histories, but exhibit the same literary phenomena, results in manifest absurdities."12

The Dead Sea Scroll communities have demonstrated the tremendous compulsion of the Hebrew people to preserve their sacred records. This they have done assiduously through the centuries. These documents were not merely legends and traditions that grew with the telling around campfires that burned constantly across the centuries. They were committed to writing as "holy men of God were inspired by

Professor Wright, photographed at the Gezer excavation by Dr. Clifford Wilson.

God's Holy Spirit" (2 Pet. 1:21). Those men of God often did not even understand everything they wrote (as 1 Pet. 1:11 tells us), but write they did.

Generations, even centuries, passed after much of that material was written, and some words, expressions, and place names in the records became obsolete. However, such reverence was shown towards those records that even the obsolescences were usually retained, assuring us who belong to the modern 20th century that the Bible writings really did date to the times claimed.

Sometimes a measure of modernization of personal and place names took place (as we today would put James instead of Jacob). Even this was often not the case, for the pattern was usually for an editing note to be added, with the original word retained. An example is at Genesis 14:3, "The vale of Siddim, which is the Salt Sea." The second clause was necessary because the encroaching waters of the Dead Sea had covered the former valley of Siddim (SDM = Sodom).

Thus, we find that sometimes the editing included a further comment or explanation. New circumstances made this desirable for the text to be understood by the later generation with whom the later compiler himself was contemporary.

If it be argued that this over-simplifies matters, we ask, "Why should it not be simple?" The highly complex Documentary Hypothesis has been disproved. Other nations had their written records. Why not the Hebrews with whom they were contemporary?

Perhaps the fact is that many scholars "having ears they do not hear, and having eyes they do not see." The evidence is there, and the stones are crying out. It is also true that a lie and a deception is often more likely to be believed than the straightforward truth. Thus, it is probable that the Documentary Hypothesis will continue to be revised, adapted, and adjusted despite the new evidence that continues to pour in against it. It is sad to contemplate, for this constant new evidence can be a clear confirmation of the wonderful fact that God has revealed himself through the centuries in the document we now know as the Bible, His Word of truth.

Ultimately the Bible itself is far more important than all the confirming evidences as to its accuracy and its integrity. It is more than a mere textbook of ancient history: it is the record of the developing revelation of God in Christ. He himself is the truth — for He declared, "I am the way, the truth and the life: no man comes to the Father except by Me" (John 14:6).

He came, He died, and He conquered, for He rose again. His victory over death was foretold by Old Testament writers and verified by New Testament men of God. His death opened the way back to God, for the gift of God is eternal life through Jesus Christ our Lord (Rom. 6:23). Individually we need to confess our shortcomings, our sins, and invite into our lives Him who bore the penalty for our sins. He lives, and He assures us, "the one who comes to Me I will by no means cast out" (John 6:37).

He himself is the central theme of God's Word of truth. The historical evidences and the archaeological confirmations are highly relevant, for they point beyond themselves to Him, the One to whom all the prophets give witness (Acts 10:43).

Moses in Egypt

A Final Brief Survey of Some Important Points.

Moses was trained in an Egyptian palace, being known by some palace officials even after he was absent for 40 years. He was indeed "instructed in all the wisdom of the Egyptians" (Acts 7:22) and was God's chosen man to establish Israel in a new way.

Under god, he pronounced judgments against the Egyptians, all of which came to pass. They served to discredit all the gods of Egypt.

At their termination the "Passover" was instituted and the Hebrews left Egypt. They miraculously passed through the Red Sea, pursued by the Egyptians who drowned when the waters returned and covered them.

In their wilderness journeys the Israelites had testings and remarkable experiences with God. The Lord provided for them by manna and water, and gave them a marvelous code of laws.

The Exodus under Moses was possibly in 1447 B.C., Thutmose III being the pharaoh of the Exodus. Moses did not introduce monotheism, but he did much to ensure its spiritual acceptance by Israel. Moses preceded (not succeeded) the heretical Pharaoh Ikhnaten who proclaimed that only he and the sun god should be worshiped. This was diametrically different from the teaching of Moses who demanded that only Jehovah should be worshiped. Moses did NOT borrow monotheism from Ikhnaten.

In Moses' law code there are some similarities to the Code of Hammurabi — such as the regulations beginning at Exodus 21:28, in relation to an ox goring a man. Moses did not need divine revelation when dealing with such everyday matters, but when dealing with moral and spiritual issues his superiority was pronounced. His laws were inspired of God.

Recovered Hittite Suzerainty Treaties make it clear that Moses' law followed a pattern of six forms that were common to his background. The researches of Professor George Mendenhall have shown that the covenant documents in the law of Moses must be dated to "the middle of the second millennium B.C." (= about 1500 B.C., the time of Moses), and were a unity.

Who but Moses was qualified to write these law codes and divine instructions? He probably used Aaron as his amanuensis (scribe) for priestly writings, and Joshua for the military strands. This would explain the legitimate use of other hands that are seen at a number of points.

SECTION III

JOSHUA AND THE CONQUEST OF CANAAN

Introduction

Joshua had been the servant of Moses, but now he takes over as leader. Immediately he is challenged by the Lord to be strong, courageous, and do everything according to all the law which Moses had commanded him (Josh. 1:6-7).

Like Moses he was a strong leader, and was largely successful in keeping the people united in their walk with Jehovah. After his death there were a number of judges, conditions quickly deteriorated to a point where "every man did what seemed right in his own eyes" (Judg. 17:6).

Joshua was very successful as a military leader with three major thrusts as he conquered the Canaanites who occupied the land. There was a campaign in the center of the land, starting with Jericho; then he went to the south, especially against Lachish and other cities; after that he proceeded to the north, especially against a confederation centered on Hazor, with great success.

Problems with the Canaanites

There were serious problems because of Canaanite religious practices which were abominable to Jehovah. At the end of his life, in a formal address, Joshua challenged the people,

> Now therefore, fear the Lord, serve Him in sincerity and in truth, and put away the gods which your fathers served on the other side of the River and in Egypt. Serve the Lord! . . . Choose for yourselves this day whom you will serve. . . . But as for me and my house, we will serve the Lord (Josh. 24:14-15).

Joshua set a high standard against these idolaters, and his influence was such that:

> The people served the Lord all the days of Joshua, and all the days of the elders who outlived Joshua, who had seen all the great works of the Lord which He had done for Israel. . . . Now Joshua . . . died. . . . When all that generation had been gathered to their fathers, another generation arose after them who did not know the Lord nor the work which He had done for Israel (Judg. 2:7-10).

Moses had died . . . and Joshua had now died . . . and their strong leadership was sadly missed. That becomes clear as we go beyond Joshua to the dark days of the judges.

Walled Cities
of the Canaanites

We learn from the Book of Numbers that the Lord told Moses to send spies to search the land, and they did so. When they returned they said that the people were strong, and the cities were walled and very great. At this time walled cities were relatively common, and a number have been excavated. The spies said they were walled up to heaven — a legitimate use of hyperbole (exaggeration) for emphasis.

The Lord sent hornets to drive out the inhabitants of the land. Possibly they were "natural" hornets, but it is also possible that it refers to the softening-up process from the Egyptian army, for the hornet was at times one of their symbols. Some of the Canaanite cities had experienced the power of the Egyptians against them, not long before the Conquest.

The people were enjoined not to rebel against the Lord or to fear the people of the land: the Lord himself was with them. In the days of the strong leader Joshua, they found the reality of the Lord's promises, but it is a sad fact that after he died there were times of weak leadership and consequent oppression.

WALLED CITIES, GRASSHOPPERS AND HORNETS (SCRIPTURE REFERENCES).

"THE LORD SPAKE UNTO MOSES SAYING – SEND THOU MEN THAT THEY MAY SEARCH THE LAND OF CANAAN."
NUMBERS 13:1

"AND THEY RETURNED ... AND SAID ...THE PEOPLE BE STRONG THAT DWELL IN THE LAND AND THE CITIES ARE WALLED AND VERY GREAT."
NUMBERS 13:28

"AND THERE WERE GIANTS ..... WE WERE IN OUR OWN SIGHT AS GRASSHOPPERS AND SO WE WERE IN THEIR SIGHT."
NUMBERS 13:33

"THE PEOPLE IS GREATER AND TALLER THAN WE: THE CITIES ARE GREAT AND WALLED UP TO HEAVEN."
DEUT 1:28

"I WILL SEND HORNETS BEFORE THEE, WHICH SHALL DRIVE OUT THE HIVITE, THE CANAANITE AND THE HITTITE."
EXODUS 23:28

"I SENT THE HORNET BEFORE YOU WHICH DRAVE THEM OUT ...BUT NOT WITH THY SWORD NOR WITH THY BOW."
JOSHUA 24:12

"REBEL NOT YE AGAINST THE LORD, NEITHER FEAR YE THE PEOPLE OF THE LAND, FOR THEY ARE BREAD FOR US, AND THE LORD IS WITH US."
NUMBERS 14:9

The Israelite spies reported that the cities were great, walled to heaven. This was a time when walled cities would have been built. This was not always the case, and the description fits the background.

Jericho Reconstructed

This is a reconstruction of Jericho as Professor Garstang thought it was like in the days of Joshua, with double walls and a palace. Possibly that part of a wooden structure across one section of the walls was where the house of Rahab was situated.

The reconstruction of Jericho on the previous page shows double walls — and one small section indicated there had been double walls. There was even evidence of a wooden structure at the top — possibly where the house of Rahab had stood. Notice that there was only one gate, and the Bible talks about the time of the shutting of the gate (Josh. 2:5).

The record also talks about "the king of Jericho," and at the time of the Conquest there were relatively small cities, each having its own king. That is the pattern given in the Bible, as can be seen in the list of kings of cities at Joshua 12:7-24. From the story of the destruction of Jericho we learn that there was a king of that one city, though it was only about seven acres in area — we read that "the king of Jericho" was told that the Israelite spies had entered the city. The casual references to kings of single cities such as Jericho, Hazor, and Lachish fit the local background and time of Joshua's day.

The River Jordan

The circuitous River Jordan had to be crossed by the Israelites. It was a great challenge to faith when Joshua was told, "Moses My servant is dead; Now therefore, arise, go over this Jordan" (Josh. 1:2). He obeyed and his faith was rewarded.

The word Jordan means "the Descender," probably because of the rapid way the stream descends. Its depth varies from about 3 feet at some fords to about 12 feet. In the 65 miles of the Upper Jordan, the descent is actually 610 feet, which is an average of about 14 feet for every mile. The Jordan surrounds are not thickly populated, partly because of the intense heat in this area which is part of the Great Rift Valley, the lowest point on earth.

In Scripture the River Jordan is important as a boundary (see Gen. 32:10; Deut. 3:20; 27:4; Josh. 1:2; Num. 34:10-12). It was also something of a military frontier, as shown at Judges 7:24 and 12:5. Many remarkable events of Scripture are associated with the Jordan, one being when Joshua led Israel across it when it was in flood, into the Promised Land. It was also well-known in association with both Elijah and

Another View of the River Jordan

The Jordan was not especially wide except in the time of harvest, which was now the case. Yet Joshua was assured that they would cross over the river on dry ground, and they did.

Elisha when each of them parted it by miraculous power, and the Syrian official Naaman was healed of his leprosy when he bathed seven times in its water.

We also read of King David crossing the Jordan in escaping from his rebellious son Absalom. And of course the Jordan is important because our Lord was baptized there by John the Baptist who was preaching in the general area.

The People Were to Cross on Dry Ground

The River Jordan is normally in flood once a year and at that time its depth and breadth are greatly increased — sometimes between 200 yards to a mile across. That is the implication of what we read as to the river being in flood once a year (see Josh. 3:4 and Eccles. 24:26).

The priests were to carry the ark of the covenant and stand in the waters at the edge of the Jordan (Josh. 3:8). At that very moment the Lord would honor their faith, and the waters that came down from upstream would be cut off and stand as a heap (verse 13). This was to be a sign to Israel that the Lord, the living God, was with them, and that He would drive out their enemies before them (verse 9).

They saw the wonder of God's Word being fulfilled — but how quickly they forgot the evidences of their own eyes! That is a continuing challenge to us who are Christians today.

The River Jordan Dammed Up

The waters which came down from upstream stood still, and rose in a heap very far away at Adam, the city that is beside Zaretan. So the waters that went down into the Sea of the Arabah, the Salt Sea, failed, and were cut off; and the people crossed over opposite Jericho (Josh. 3:16).

It is a historical fact that at times the River Jordan has been blocked up at the site of Adam (the modern Damieh). Thus it was dammed up for 16 hours in A.D. 1267, and Professor John Garstang reported a similar happening for 21 hours in 1927 — and there have been other similar reports. Possibly that was the means by which God caused the Jordan River to stop flowing at the time of Joshua, for He controls the forces of nature.

The Jordan at Damieh

Adam (the modern Damieh) about 18 miles north of Jericho is believed to be where the Jordan was dammed up in Joshua's day. Similar damming has taken place several times in known history. Possibly God used the forces of nature with a landslide.

Miracles at times involve the actual timing of events, but whatever the explanation, it is clear that God saw to it that His people would cross this extensive body of water as dry land. His people's faith had to be demonstrated and then, as the priests put their feet towards the water, it was seen that God was indeed in control with this miraculous damming up of the water for some 18 miles.

Clay Tablet Is from Amarna

In 1887 a peasant woman in Egypt found some 300 cuneiform tablets at Amarna. They basically were appeals from various princes in Palestine/Syria to the then reigning Egyptian pharaoh, somewhere about 1400 to 1360 B.C., asking for help against invaders who were known as Habiru. It seems that there were other invaders besides the Habiru, and although at times some scholars have identified the Hebrews with these people, it seems more likely that they could have been among the invaders — i.e., only part of the whole. Many scholars believe that the Habiru were not only Hebrews. However, the question is still a matter of debate.

Amarna was an important political religious and cultural

Tablets in ancient Amarna near the Nile in Egypt were discovered by a peasant woman in the late 19th century. They are an interesting background to the situation in Canaan at about the time of the Conquest by the Israelites.

center about the time of the Hebrew Exodus from Egypt. It was brought to greater prominence by the pharaoh whom later Egyptians regarded as a heretic — Amenhotep IV, who changed his name to Ikhnaton. He claimed that the sun god Aton was the only god, and that he himself was the living manifestation of that god. Some claim that this was a form of monotheism but it was merely a way of having himself honored as the only god. His teaching was dramatically different from the monotheism and the holiness associated with it as taught by the great man Moses.

Amarna was renamed Akhetaton, meaning city of Aton. However, Ikhnaton's religious teachings were abandoned only a few years after his death. Egypt reverted to its previous gross polytheism. Dr. Howard Vos says in his *Archaeology and Bible Lands*:

> If one holds to the early date of the Exodus, the Amarna Letters may reflect the unsettled conditions during or shortly after the time of the Conquest. But it is too much to say that the Amarna Letters are merely the Canaanite form of the biblical account of the Conquest.[13]

Excavation at Jericho

This is the general area where Dr. Kathleen Kenyon excavated. She rejected the biblical claims about Jericho, but later researchers have shown that some of her own findings actually fit in with the biblical story.

Dr. Kathleen Kenyon excavated in this part of Jericho from 1952 to 1958 as director of the British School of Archaeology in Jerusalem. The excavation was jointly sponsored by the British School and the American Schools of Oriental Research.

Dr. Kenyon was very critical of the earlier work of Sir John Garstang, especially of his conclusions relating to the walls of Jericho in Joshua's day. She concluded that they were made of mud brick, and that they would have eroded away during the centuries when the site was unoccupied. However, Dr. Kenyon excavated only a small part of Jericho, and her somewhat sweeping conclusions were based on insufficient evidence. She possibly confused minimal remains that were left later by the troops of King Eglon of Moab (Judg. 3:13) with the earlier conquest by Joshua.

In the light of more recent evidence there has been a swing back to the conclusions of Sir John Garstang, though not at every point. Dr. Kenyon's conclusions, and even her dating, have been seriously challenged. Dr. Bryant Wood has been a leader in this challenge to the dating of Jericho's destruction, but there have been wider criticisms that Kenyon (wrongly) concluded too much from very small areas excavated at both Jericho and Jerusalem.[14]

John Ankerberg at Jericho

John Ankerberg stands with his daughter Michelle above the Kenyon trench at Jericho. "The John Ankerberg Show" is well-known in America for its consistent defense of the Scriptures.

Here John Ankerberg, with his daughter Michelle, is at the site of ancient Jericho. It looks as if he is standing on the wall, but in fact he is not. The Scriptures declare that the walls of Jericho fell down at the time of Joshua's attack, and what looks like a wall is actually a reminder that ancient sites have been lived in at various time periods, covering several levels of occupation.

Nevertheless, the walls would have been even higher than what we see in this picture. Some of these Canaanite walls were 30 feet high, even having towers estimated at about 60 feet high. It is little wonder, humanly speaking, that ten of the spies who returned from Canaan were frightened. They declared that the walls were great and walled up to heaven.

The Bible record about the destruction of this ancient city continues to be vindicated. As Dr. John J. Bimson states, "In the case of Jericho we have archaeological evidence for plague, earthquake, and the deliberate destruction of the city by fire, each of which is attested in the narrative."[15]

The "Neolithic" Tower at Jericho

*This is said to be one of the world's oldest structures of the so-called Neolithic (New Stone) Age —
supposedly dated to 7000 B.C. Kathleen Kenyon showed that man's food-gathering and food-producing
stages were recent and contemporary.*

One good result of Dr. Kenyon's work was her uncovering of the famous "Neolithic Tower," which she dated to about 7000 B.C. — about as early as the original settlement of this, one of the oldest cities in the world.

We note that no dating is necessarily conclusive before the time of the biblical flood because of the dramatic atmospheric changes which appear to have taken place at that time. Instead of constants, the data before that time would involve a series of variables, and conclusions about ages are therefore unreliable.

Nevertheless, Dr. Kenyon made an important contribution by showing that food gathering and food producing were undertaken at the same time, and not separated by thousands of years. Mankind was not just nomadic for vast periods of time until some of their numbers began to produce crops — the two areas of activity went on side by side, as the evidence at Jericho indicated.

The early chapters of Genesis indicate that so-called "early" man was highly intelligent, with various forms of activity being contemporaneous. Dr. Kenyon's conclusion fits with the biblical evidence at this point.

The Temptation of Our Lord

When Satan tested Jesus, he distorted the Word of God. In one temptation he misquoted Scripture by leaving out the important words "In all your ways."

For He shall give His angels charge over you, To keep you in all your ways. In their

Jericho and the Mount of Temptation

Traditionally Jesus looked down from this mountain at the time when Satan tempted Him by offering Him all the world.

hands they shall bear you up, Lest you dash your foot against a stone (Ps. 91:11-12).

If Jesus had cast himself over the temple, as Satan desired, he would have been outside the will of His Father. We have no right to break laws (such as speeding), but are to ensure that our walk with God is pleasing to Him — "In all your ways."

Satan also offered Jesus all the kingdom of the world — provided He would fall down and worship Satan, thus making Satan's victory complete. The offer was made on a mountain, and tradition says it was made on this one outside Jericho. If so, Jesus would have looked down on Jericho, one of the oldest cities in the world. Obviously He did not succumb to the deceitful wiles of the devil.

Burnt Wheat from Jericho

When the English archaeologist Professor Sir John Garstang excavated at Jericho, he reported the finding of what appeared to be a royal palace. In it there were various foods burned, including quantities of wheat. The city had been destroyed by fire, just as we read in Joshua 6:24:

> But they burned the city and all that was in it with fire. Only the silver and gold, and the vessels of bronze and iron, they put into the treasury of the house of the Lord.

Despite the challenges from Dame Kathleen Kenyon against the earlier findings of Sir John Garstang, her own excavation conclusions have now been seriously challenged at a number of points, and those of Sir John Garstang have been largely (not

This wheat was part of the vast quantities of burnt food Sir John Garstang found when he excavated Jericho. Despite Kenyon's later criticisms, his work still largely demonstrates the authenticity of the destruction of Jericho in the days of Joshua.

entirely) re-instated. The Bible record of the destruction of Jericho has stood secure, despite hammering blasts of critics over the last generation.

As stated above, the researches of Dr. Bryant Wood have done much to show that the Bible record of Joshua must be taken literally as a first-class historical record. This burnt wheat from the palace is another testimony to the factual nature of the biblical record.

Bones and Pottery at Jericho

The Australian Institute of Archaeology contributed financially to the excavation of Jericho. This burial jar, bones and all, is part of their display in Melbourne.

Living people were at times buried in foundations of temples and other buildings. Burning was another means of human sacrifice to Canaanite deities. Canaanite religious practices in these and other ways were an abomination to God.

The Canaanite cup of iniquity was full, and the time of judgment had come. One important point, which is often overlooked when the question about the destruction of the Canaanites is asked, is that the concept of God being associated with love is a Bible concept anyhow. Other nations certainly did not think of "love" in association with their gods. God in His love had been longsuffering towards these people, and only when His mercy was finally rejected did He act in judgment towards them. The Hebrews were His instrument.

Throughout the Scriptures this is constantly shown as a principle of God's dealings with men. He waited in the days of Noah, but eventually He acted in judgment. He waited in the days of Egypt's oppression, but eventually those who rejected Him were also judged. In the days of Noah, salvation was provided for those who would heed God's warnings. Now God's judgment was being executed against the depraved Canaanites.

Children's Bones at Jericho

This funerary jar contained the bones of children, buried beneath one of the structures at Jericho. It also is from the collection of the Australian Institute of Archaeology. These bones remind us that children were at times offered as sacrifices to the gods, and the Canaanite practices associated with their idol worship were abominable. Children and others were sacrificed to Baal and Asherah (there are variations of her name) and other Canaanite deities.

The worship of Canaanite gods and the related practices were serious problems to the Israelites. There were surface similarities between the two religions, with animal and bird sacrifices. However, they were only surface likenesses. Concepts such as holiness and righteousness were unknown to the evil powers whom the Canaanites worshiped.

As we have seen, the abominations associated with Canaanite religion were of such a nature that God ordered their destruction. Their "cup of iniquity" was full and there was a very real danger of their being like a cancer in the midst of Israel.

The Canaanites attempted to PLACATE their evil deities by sacrifices such as these. The Israelites were called to WORSHIP the one true God, Jehovah.

Pottery Evidence from Jericho

Pottery evidence such as this from Jericho has been the subject of much controversy. Dr. Kathleen Kenyon excavated and radically disagreed with some of the dating and other conclusions of earlier excavations by Sir John Garstang.

However, Kenyon's own conclusions (both as to her work at Jerusalem and at Jericho) have come under attack, it being claimed that she made far-reaching conclusions that were not justified by the findings in the small areas she excavated at both places. In addition, some of her work (published

Pottery from Jericho has been re-interpreted with modern dating and other techniques, by highly qualified Dr. Bryant Wood. He concludes that Jericho was destroyed about 1400 B.C., the "early" biblical date for the beginning of the Conquest.

after her death) gives a pottery date of 1400 for Jericho's destruction — thus at least in that specific conclusion agreeing with the recognized "early" date for the Conquest, commencing about 1400 B.C.[16]

Now Dr. Bryant Wood has undertaken considerable research on the Jericho pottery stored in England and the USA, and he has shown by modern dating methods that Kenyon simply made mistakes in much of her dating. Dr. Wood concludes that Jericho fell about 1400 B.C., fitting the view held by many conservative biblical scholars. (To the personal knowledge of this writer, Dr. Clifford Wilson, a cache of Philistine pots found at Gezer in 1969 was 150 years "out," possibly pointing to that early date again.)

The God Baal of the Canaanites

Today, more than 3,000 years after the conquest of Canaan, the name "Baal" is still a synonym for that which is opposed to God. This is because Scripture makes it clear that the worship of Baal was repugnant to Jehovah, and the chosen people were constantly urged to withdraw from all association with Baal and the other Canaanite deities.

The word "Baal" actually means "master" or "lord," and as such, the Canaanites used this term to apply to various gods, including the well-known storm god Hadad. This absorption of other deities was essentially different from the Israelite approach to their God, for they were expressly warned that he was "a jealous God."

In addition to the father-figure El who was regarded as being in the distant heavens (too far removed to be actively involved in the affairs of mankind), Baal and Asherah were the principal god and goddess of the Canaanites. Baal was essentially associated with the sun, storms, and other aspects of nature worship, whereas Asherah was more directly linked with sex and fertility. The worship associated with both deities was both grossly licentious and extremely cruel.

The Goddess Asherah of the Canaanites

Although there is some confusion about the inter-relationship of Canaanite deities, it seems likely that Asherah was the wife of the chief god El, the father god who did not come down into the affairs of men. She was apparently also the wife of Baal, as well as being his mother. Canaanite deities, including this one, had a great love for human blood.

The goddess Anath is described as wading in human blood to her knees and then to her thighs. She cut off the heads of many of her victims, and tied them as adornments for her back, with many of her victims' hands tied on her belt. In all this, according to the Baal epic, her liver was swollen with laughter, her joy was great, and she was full of exaltation. She even washed her hands in human blood before she turned to other activities. (Anath is an alternative name

It seems that Baal's wife was Asherah, who was also the consort of El, the father god: the precise relationship is complicated. Asherah's rituals were depraved, and we now understand why God ordered the destruction of the Canaanites.

for the goddess Asherah; some scholars believe that Ashtaroth is another.)

The Children of Israel were in spiritual danger from the Canaanite religious practices, especially in regards to those which bore similarities to Israelite offerings. Baal and Asherah fit the biblical description of false angels of light in the background of Israelite life.

The Retirement Home of David Ben-Gurion

Israel's first prime minister in modern times, David Ben-Gurion, lived here in retirement. The humble cottage was in keeping with the nature of the man himself. (A copy of Hal Lindsey's Late Great Planet Earth *is displayed in his book-case.)*

The humble cottage at Sede-Boker ("Rancher's Field"), about 11 miles south of Jerusalem was the retirement home of David Ben-Gurion. He was Israel's first prime minister when Israel's new nationhood was declared in May 1948. Clearly he did not seek personal wealth or great areas of land for himself. The former David Green became David Ben-Gurion — Ben denoting "son of," and his Western name Green was Hebraized to Gurion.

Many Bible scholars believe that David Ben-Gurion was a servant of God in the sense that King Cyrus of Persia had been over 2,500 years earlier. Isaiah the prophet had predictively declared that Cyrus would be called of the Lord by name, to fulfill His purposes for Israel (Isa. 45:4). The Lord is ever in control of the nations and His purposes are sure — being known to Him forever. Cyrus declared that the people of Israel could return from captivity — at a specific time, which also had been declared by God (Jer. 25:12; 29:10).

In modern times Israel has again been declared a nation, even though, humanly speaking, such a prospect seemed impossible. And David Ben-Gurion was a statesman and leader in that dramatic series of happenings.

A View from David Ben-Gurion's Home

The rugged area around the home of the late David Ben-Gurion is a constant reminder of the early history of his people as they marched into Canaan about 3,400 years ago. In the days of Abraham it was

A View from the Home of David Ben-Gurion

As they marched through this southern area the Israelites were a terror to the people throughout the land. The Israelites knew the wonder of God's presence.

possible to move fairly freely through the area, for occupation was much more sparse then than it was in the days of the Conquest by Joshua.

Now Joshua's men would come up against defense systems that were carefully planned. Many of their enemies had iron chariots, and these were of course quite foreign to the Israelites. They moved on foot, and their God-given task was certainly not an easy one by human standards. They had spent their whole lives in a quite different type of country — they were, literally, a wilderness people. Except for Joshua and Caleb the whole of the older generation that had come out of Egypt had died.

What hope did they have against chariots? How could they ever hope to defeat well-armed troops coming out from awe-inspiring "cities walled up to heaven"? How could they defeat the Canaanites who had "modern" fighting equipment which would have been way ahead of the implements available to Joshua's army? The answer is that God was with them — and the victories were assured while they walked with God.

Perhaps David Ben-Gurion's people also knew something of the power of that same great God as they were attacked by the surrounding nations in 1948 (and in later years).

We have already referred to the fact that Joshua's troops would have come marching through the southern areas of Canaan, and we have put forward the date of about 1400 B.C. for the commencement of the Conquest (not 1240 B.C., the "late date" of some modern scholars).

One argument for that late (1240 B.C.) date is that Pharaohs Thutmose III and Amenhotep II were located at Thebes, not at the abandoned city of Memphis which was relatively close to Goshen in the Delta region where the Hebrews lived. However, a recovered scarab shows that Amenhotep II was actually born at Memphis, indicating a royal presence there, rather than it being an abandoned city in his time.

Another major argument for the late date is that no archaeological evidence has been forthcoming to show that some of the cities destroyed by Joshua were actually destroyed by fire. However, the Bible does not state that Joshua burnt all the cities he conquered. In fact, after burning the ones he first conquered he seems to have had a change of policy, with cities left standing on their tells ("mounds" — see Josh. 11:13). The inhabitants of various cities were destroyed (Josh. 10:38-39) but not necessarily the actual cities. A good example is Debir which was conquered by Joshua (Josh. 10:38-39). It was apparently re-occupied by the Canaanites who in turn saw it defeated a second time by Othniel, the nephew of Caleb (Josh. 15:15-17).

The Graves of David and Paula Ben-Gurion

David Ben-Gurion, Israel's founding prime minister in modern times, is buried here, with his wife, Paula, alongside him.

The place is something of a shrine for the people of Israel. David Ben-Gurion was very much a father figure to his people. That was demonstrated even by his coming to Sede-Boker on his retirement, sharing with others of varied backgrounds in their desire to reclaim this wilderness area of the Negev.

David Ben-Gurion is buried in front of his modest retirement home. Mrs. Paula Ben-Gurion is buried alongside him. The people of Israel have great memories of this one whom they regard as a beloved father figure in their new nationhood.

Later he was recalled to the Kenesset, and again became prime minister of Israel for a time.

David Ben-Gurion was a great statesman, and a man who claimed to honor the God of his fathers.

Another View of the Southern Terrain

As Joshua and his men traversed this southern terrain, they would have had the confident knowledge that the Lord was with them. They had seen the marvel of His presence with them as they crossed the River Jordan on dry land. They had seen his hand at Jericho, they had seen the wonder of the Captain of the host leading them, they had known his victorious presence as they fought against the assembled kings at Gibeon, and now they were to engage in the southern campaign.

They had even seen the marvel of God fighting for them with the very forces of nature on their side — hailstones being part of the method the Lord used, as shown at Joshua 10:11 — "The Lord cast down great stones from heaven on them unto Azekah, and they died." Their trust was in the Lord, and further events were to prove that that trust was not misplaced.

So they marched through the wilderness areas with confidence, their hearts singing because they knew they would triumph against the Canaanites whose cup of iniquity was full. Their enemies had blatantly rejected the standards of Jehovah as they insisted on going on with abominations associated with their worship of Baal and Asherah.

The modern tourists in our picture are marching through the wilderness in the general area of the retirement home of the late David Ben-Gurion. It is easy to imagine the troops of Joshua marching through territory such as this, throughout the land, as they approached the walled cities of the Canaanites. God was surely with them, as is made clear by the rapid nature of their conquests.

Joshua's Capture of Lachish

The modern name of Lachish is Tell-ed-Duweir, about 30 miles southwest of Jerusalem. Jerome Murphy-O'Connor (in his *The Holy Land: An Archaeological Guide from Earliest Times to 1700*) comments on it being "a very deceptive site . . . it is only when one stands on top that the authority of its situation becomes apparent." The view to west, north, and east is magnificent. "Canaanite cities had existed on the mound for almost 3,000 years before it was taken by Joshua." He further refers to a Canaanite temple having been discovered.[17]

Joshua 10:31-33 records that Joshua and his troops captured Lachish. When excavation revealed that the city was destroyed by fire about 1230 B.C., with an inscribed bowl and a scarab of Pharaoh Raamses II being found, many scholars decided that this was the destruction by Joshua, confirming the so-called late date for the Exodus and the Conquest by the Israelites.

The Southern City of Lachish

Joshua and his troops were victorious against the southern city of Lachish after they had been so successful in the conquest in the center of the land, where cities such as Jericho had been destroyed. The king of Lachish was hanged.

However, as Merrill F. Unger says in his *Archaeology and the Old Testament*, "Besides being completely out of focus with the findings at Jericho and the general biblical datings the fact must be faced that the biblical record says not a word about the city itself being burned or destroyed when taken by Joshua."[18] In fact, Joshua 11:13 makes it clear that Joshua's later policy was NOT to burn cities but to leave them standing. The Lord himself fought for Joshua, and that explains the rapid nature of the Conquest, including the capture of Lachish (here pictured) in the south.

The Canaanite City of Hazor

Joshua's northern campaign centered around the city of Hazor, pictured on the following page, with ruins dating to about the time of Solomon and earlier.

There is a fascinating story as to the finding and identification of this city of Hazor in modern times. Professor John Garstang saw the site below him one morning, having set out with the deliberate intention of finding Hazor from the clues given in the Bible. He describes his own excitement when he localized and identified the lost site which had been so famous in Israel's history. In later times the site was excavated, and Garstang's identification was shown to be correct — and the clues from the Bible were vindicated.

Hazor was one of the greatest cities of ancient times in all Palestine and Assyria. It could have had a

Hazor, to the North

After the conquest in the central and southern parts of the land, Joshua and his men had to fight against a coalition of kings centered at Hazor in the north. This particular view of Hazor is at a somewhat later time, but the location is the same.

population of over 40,000 people, and certainly could have raised a large force. That is the picture implicit in the record about this city, in Joshua 11. There we read that Hazor was the leading city among all those in the north of Israel.

King Jabin of Hazor?

When Joshua attacked the city of Hazor in the north, he defeated a coalition of several kings. The king of Hazor was named Jabin, and it is believed that this is a statue of that king. When Joshua destroyed the city, a Canaanite temple was included in the destruction, and this figure was among those recovered.

It appears to be of a royal person, and presumably it was a statue of the king who was reigning at the time of Joshua's attack. The fact of destruction suggests it was the Jabin of Joshua's time, and not the later King Jabin mentioned in Judges 4:2. The description in Joshua 11 mentions King Jabin who was defeated at the time of Joshua's campaign. A third Jabin is now known from arachaeology.

In the battle against Jabin and his associates, humanly speaking, Joshua should have been defeated. However, Joshua was fighting in the strength of the Captain of the host who had met him outside Jericho, soon after the Israelites crossed the Jordan River into the land of Canaan. His victory was assured!

Megiddo

Joshua's troops came against Megiddo, but at first they were unable to conquer it. The Israelites, fresh from the desert, needed the supernatural power of God to be victorious against the advanced technology of some of their opponents.

Megiddo was one of the most ancient cities in the Promised Land. It commanded the strategic highway that led from Egypt right through to the north of Canaan. Many battles were fought there throughout history, including a campaign against the Canaanites led by Thutmose III, the king of Egypt who was probably the pharaoh of the Exodus. Even in modern times there have been various battles associated with Megiddo. General Allenby captured the city in World War I, and the Israel forces took it in 1948.

Dr. John Bimson gives technical data (based on pottery and other evidence) to indicate that there is no established basis for the widely held view that Thutmose actually destroyed Megiddo. Megiddo was fortified by King Solomon, along with Gezer and Hazor.

Model of Megiddo

Megiddo is somewhat of a showpiece for archaeological work in Israel. There were about 20 levels at this site, and here Israeli guide Benjamin Shavit is lecturing about some of the important facts now known from excavation.

The various levels of the model can be moved up and down so that a particular time level can be looked at closely, helped by lights and other modern teaching aids. Careful reconstruction makes it possible for the scholar — or the tourist — to understand technical aspects by firsthand examination.

There were four temples revealed by excavation, with the oldest of them supposedly dating to about 3000 B.C., including a circular altar over 25 feet in diameter. Organized religious practices were known very early in man's settled civilizations.

Israel Guide Ben
Jamin Shavit
Alongside Megiddo
Model

*The Megiddo model at the
site is remarkable (though
challengeable as to the
dating of some time
periods). The many levels
of occupation can be
looked at separately by
winding them up or down
according to
requirements.*

However, there is still considerable debate about the dating of some levels. Dr. John Bimson is one scholar who discusses this in some detail — he states, for example, "We must conclude that no archaeological reason has been produced for placing the events of Judges 4 - 5 in the 12th century B.C."[19] The straightforward dates of the Bible continue to stand investigation better than opposing dates do.

Entering the Water Tunnel at Megiddo

The water system at this ancient site of Megiddo was one of the most impressive in all of the land of Canaan. The Canaanite engineers cut through the solid rock as they tunneled through the rock to a spring that was located outside the city. They actually covered the spring so that any attackers would not suspect that there was a shaft leading into the city.

At Megiddo the shaft itself is about 80 feet deep and the tunnel is 224 feet long. Indentations on the wall indicate that the original Canaanite workers moved towards each other from opposite ends. The tunnel was greatly improved by the Israelites in the days of King Ahab.

Joshua had great difficulty with some of the Canaanites because they had "chariots of iron" (Josh. 17:18). When we see their engineering achievements, such as with their water tunnels, we certainly can understand this other special technical ability also.

The Megiddo Water Shaft Today

The water shaft led through the rock to a spring outside the walled city itself. As necessary, the spring would be covered so that an attacking enemy would not know of its existence. Canaanite engineers often showed considerable ingenuity in the way they ensured the safety of their so-necessary water supply.

In times of war, water would be available to the inhabitants inside the city. When peace reigned there would be easier access to the spring outside the city, without fear of enemy interference.

Similar water tunnels are known in other ancient Canaanite cities, notably Hazor and Gezer. They were an important part of the defense systems of these Canaanite cities also.

The wooden platform in this picture has been constructed in recent times over the water level of the ancient tunnel itself.

Canaanite Altar at Megiddo

This is the circular altar built at Megiddo not long after the city was established by the Canaanites in the third millennium B.C. It was over 25 feet in diameter and there were seven steps ascending to it — which is a different pattern from that demanded of the Israelites who were not to have steps as such leading to the altar.

In our picture two

visitors are playing out a drama of sacrificing a human on this altar. We have seen that in the days before Joshua it was not "acting out," for such sacrifices were relatively commonplace.

In various ways Canaanite practices were serious sinful departures from the patterns that God required of His covenant people. By the time of the Conquest under Joshua their "cup of iniquity" was full, and God ordered their destruction. They were like a cancer in the midst of Israel. As a surgeon takes a knife for remedial purposes, so God ordered the destruction of these depraved people.

Humans Were Sacrificed at the Megiddo Altar

The fact of human sacrifices was all too common in Canaanite worship, and this was abominable to God: adults, children, and even babies were sacrificed. The associated religious rites were abominations before the Lord:

> You shall utterly destroy all the places wherein the nations which you shall possess serve their gods, upon the high mountains, and upon the hills, and under every green tree;
>
> And you shall overthrow their altars, and break their pillars, and burn their groves with fire; and you shall hew down the graven images of their gods, and destroy the names of them out of that place (Deut. 12:2-3).

We notice in passing that the plural word translated "groves" in the Authorized Version of the Bible is better translated as "Asherim" — now known as Canaanite deities. The word "Asherah" in various forms is actually used both for the deity and for structures associated with the worship of Asherah.

The Jezreel Valley

This is the area that stretches out from Megiddo, which is in a raised area. In "the last days" vast numbers will be gathered here, and God's judgment against the nations opposing Israel will finally be seen. The excavation is Schumaker's trench.

The Jezreel Valley

The name of Megiddo (which overlooked the Jezreel Valley) first appears on the temple of Karnak in Egypt. There the Egyptian Pharaoh Thutmose III carved a detailed record of the battle that his troops fought in the general area of Megiddo in May 1468 B.C.

To quote Murphy-O'Connor again,

> From the top of the tell . . . every movement of the swirling chariot squadrons can be plotted; that day Thutmose captured 924 enemy chariots! Six letters from its king, Biridiya, were found in the archives of the Egyptian Foreign Ministry at Amarna . . . one howling for aid against Shechem. The quality of the architecture and hordes of ivory, gold, and jewelry bear witness to the great prosperity of the city.[20]

This battle involving Pharaoh Thutmose III might have been part of the "softening-up" process against the Canaanites while the Hebrews were still in the wilderness.

Looking Across the Plain from Megiddo

Megiddo was actually at the southern edge of the Plain of Jezreel. The city wall extended right around the mound, measuring approximately 890 yards and being about 11 feet thick in most places.

As Jerome Murphy-O'Connor says:

> From time immemorial armies have surged from the surrounding valleys to play their parts on the flat stage of the Jezreel Valley. . . .

> Its position at the head of the most important pass through the Carmel range . . . gave Megiddo control of the Way of the Sea, the ancient trade-route between Egypt and the east. . . . Traders from all over the known world passed its gates, as did invading armies.

> Megiddo (Armageddon) will yet again be the battle ground for vast invading armies (Zech. 12:11).

Megiddo is the site referred to in both Old and New Testaments where a great battle — "the Battle of Armageddon" — is to take place. Armageddon is literally Har Megiddo — Mount Megiddo. An Israeli Air Force base is located there today.

Mount Tabor, with the Valley of Jezreel Below

As we proceed through the Book of Judges we find that the Israelites constantly reverted to worshiping Canaanite deities. However, when they repented God raised up judges (saviors) to deliver them.

Mount Tabor is where God raised up Deborah and Barak to defeat the forces of Sisera, the commander of the Canaanite troops at Hazor. Despite Sisera's 900 chariots and a large army, Barak soundly defeated him with 10,000 men. Not one of Sisera's men was left, and Sisera himself was ignominiously killed by Jael, the wife of Heber the Kenite (Judg. 4:17-22).

As can be seen, the plain between Mount Tabor and Megiddo extends for many miles and it is not surprising that it is the place where yet another great battle is to take place at the end times. The word Armageddon actually is Har-Megiddon, Mount Megiddo.

John Ankerberg is host of the television's far-reaching "John Ankerberg Show" which stands strongly for the integrity of Scripture. He is here seen on Mount Tabor (the possible Mount of Transfiguration) with his wife, Darlene, and daughter Michelle.

The Plain of Jezreel

Looking down on the vast area of the plain of the valley of Jezreel from the top of Mount Tabor, we can understand some of the reason why God decreed that here a great final battle would take place. This is what we read at Revelation 16:14-16:

> For they are spirits of demons, performing signs, which go out to the kings of the earth and of the whole world, to gather them to the battle of that great day of God Almighty (Rev. 16:14).

> And they gathered them together to the place called in Hebrew, Armageddon (Rev. 16:16).

Here is another view of the Jezreel Valley stretching out from Mount Tabor. Here Deborah and Barak used thousands of troops, and clearly the possibility of vast numbers of troops being engaged in battle in this area at the end times is all too real.

At the other side of the plain, Armageddon also overlooks the Valley of Jezreel: "Armageddon" literally means Mount Megiddo. Our picture again makes it clear that vast armies could certainly be engaged in deadly battle in this part of Israel. An Israeli Air Force base is located there today.

Many biblical scholars accept the Bible's statement that this valley is to be the scene of God's judgment against the enemies of Israel in "the last days." We recognize that "the last days" is a general term stretching across a long period. Peter used it to describe events occurring in his time (Acts 2:17). We are NOT date-setting.

The Spring of Harod

Here Gideon's men came together to fight against the Midianites. Gideon was told to send home those who did not want to fight, and to take the others down to the water. God was showing that the Midianites would be overcome only by His power.

Gideon's Three Hundred Men

> Then the Lord said to Gideon, "By the three hundred men who lapped will I save you, and deliver the Midianites into your hand. Let all the other people go, every man to his place (Judg. 7:7).

This is that time when God made it clear that He would deliver the Israelites from their enemies, but they would not be dependent on their own army of thousands of men. God first had Gideon reduce his army by sending 22,000 men who were "fearful and afraid" back home, leaving only 10,000 to face the 135,000 Midianites (Judg. 7:3). Then it was further reduced to only 300 men who did not "get down on his knees to drink," but instead "lapped, putting their hand to their mouth" (Judg. 7:5-6). This is the area where the 300 men lapped.

No explanation for this choice is given. If it was not simply God's way of drastically reducing the forces used, the choice was probably based on alertness, just as the first was based on courage. The lapping was apparently from the hands rather than directly from the brook's surface.

> Then the three companies blew the trumpets and broke the pitchers — they held the torches in their left hands and the trumpets in their right hands for blowing — and they cried, "The sword of the Lord and of Gideon!" (Judg. 7:20).

As we read on we find that they were victorious against the thousands of Midianites who opposed them.

Judges 7:20 is widely known as the key motto of the Christian laymen's organization known as the Gideons. Their local chapters are known as "camps," and they have a strong emphasis on the Scriptures as "the Sword of the Spirit," able to conquer the enemy and win victories for the Lord. The event itself was a great

Those who put their mouths into the water would be totally unable to see the enemy; probably the concept of alertness was involved. Here at the Spring of Harod, Dr. Clifford Wilson is lapping with his hand, rather than putting his mouth into the water.

testimony, both for the remarkably effective victory strategy utilized by Gideon, and also for the providential working of God himself.

Although the Midianites and the Amalekites were "as numerous as locusts" (Judg. 7:12), the 300 men with the minimal equipment ordered by God inflicted a devastating defeat on them. Their faith in the true God Jehovah was vindicated — and there is an implicit challenge to ongoing faith for the Christian today.

Fighting Philistines

From inscriptions dating to the times of the judges we know a great deal about the Philistines. They wore laminated body armor, and their bodies were protected also with small round shields. They had a distinctive headdress, with feathered tiaras. Dr. Ed. Hindsen in *The Philistines in the Old Testament* makes the point that these compared with the classical illusion to the carian crest on their helmets[21] (Strabo, XIV, LI 329).

These Philistines are shown on the pylon of the Ramasseum (Egypt). They were an invading sea people who gave their name to ancient Palestine and were prominent as opponents of Israel in the later period of the judges.

The giant Philistine warrior Goliath was arrayed in typical Philistine armor, though much bigger than normal. He wore a coat of mail, with greaves of glass on his legs, and equipment such as this occurs in various depictions of the period. Goliath had a large heavy spear, with a massive iron head. The shaft was said to be like a weaver's beam, and by human standards this well-equipped warrior was totally superior to the poorly-armed Israelites — especially the stripling David!

The archaeological evidence shows that the Philistines were especially strong in the Judges period, settling in Canaan in large numbers in the 12th and 11th centuries B.C. They were able to threaten the Israelites in inland areas.

Sculpture about Samson

This sculpture at Ashkelon is a modern version of the way Samson would have brought down the temple of the Philistine corn god Dagan (not the "fish god" as previously believed).

Ashkelon is on the Mediterranean seacoast, some 12 miles north of Gaza. In ancient times

vessels came from many countries to purchase grain. Herod the Great was born here, and later he had many buildings and colonnaded streets constructed. Through the centuries various peoples were in control of Ashkelon, including the Canaanites, the Philistines, the Maccabeans, the Greeks, the Romans, later the Crusaders, and then the Arabic people. Today it is under the control of Israel.

It is clear Ashkelon and Gaza were two of five Philistine capitals in the days of the Judges. Each of these five cities had their own territory, and there were other (daughter) towns dependent on them. Relevant biblical references are Joshua 15:45-47; 1 Chronicles 18:1; 2 Samuel 1:20 and Ezekiel 16:27, 57. These people were very ready to amalgamate with other people whom they conquered, and to absorb their religion and their deities. That was shown by the fact that the Philistines took over the Canaanite temple at Beth-shean when Saul was killed on Mount Gilboa. His head was put in the Philistine temple, and his armor in the Canaanite temple.

These five prominent cities were organized as a confederacy as early as the time of Joshua: they were an amphictyonic league or state (a group bound together by some common interest, often religious). The Bible writers consistently recognized the dominance of these five cities, as shown in such references as that to Gaza (Josh. 13:3 and Amos 1:7-8). At 1 Samuel 6:17 there is a reference to Ashdod which seems to indicate that this city was the recognized religious center. In the biblical lists Ekron is always put last, with the order of the three major cities of Ashdod, Gath and Ashkelon being interchangeable. In 1 Samuel 6:16-18 the five capital cities are brought together (Ashdod, Gaza, Ashkelon, Gath, and Ekron).

Samson Destroys a Philistine Temple

We read in Judges 15:20 and Judges 16:31 that Samson was a judge over Israel, his period of authority lasting for 20 years. His exploits are recorded in Judges 13 through 16. The Valley of Sorec was the scene of his major exploits, and Israeli people identify this with the Wadi El Seirar which emerges from the Judean hills about 15 miles west of Jerusalem.

Samson accomplished more in his death by the destruction of the idolatrous Philistines than he did in his disappointing life. Nevertheless Samson was a chosen man of God, and his incredible strength was more than the natural strength that the strongest of men could develop in their own bodies. The Spirit of the Lord came upon him at times, giving him supernatural strength. He was gradually able to deliver Israel (practically single-handedly) from the Philistines. That is specifically mentioned three times

This particular sculpture is on the road between Ashkelon and Tel Aviv. Ashkelon was one of the Philistine capitals. The Bible correctly identifies the five Philistine capitals of Ashdod, Gaza, Ashkelon, Gath and Ekron (see 1 Sam. 6:16-18).

(Judg. 14:6,19; 15:14), and it is implied for his other exploits as well.

Samson's greatest feat of superhuman strength was his pulling down the temple of Dagan, thereby slaying over 3,000 Philistine leaders and their people. That resulted as an answer to his final prayer to God (Judg. 16:28).

A Reminder of Another Samson — at Ephesus

Sometimes archaeological finds demonstrate biblical truth indirectly.

The story of Samson pulling down the temple of the Philistine god Dagan is well-known. In Judges we read that Samson took hold of the two middle pillars which were the mainstay of the temple building. As the story goes on we read that he bowed himself with all his might and was able to pull the building down:

> And Samson took hold of the two middle pillars which supported the temple, and he braced himself against them, one on his right and the other on his left
>
> Then Samson said, "Let me die with the Philistines!" And he pushed with all his might, and the temple fell on the lords and all the people who were in it. So the dead that he killed at his death were more than he had killed in his life (Judg. 16:29-30).

These two pillars are all that is still standing from one of the temples at Ephesus. Ephesus is the site of one of the seven churches in Revelation, chapters 2 and 3. Rev. Cliff Bennetts is standing between the two pillars: it takes little imagination to realize that a man such as Samson, with superhuman strength, could pull down the temple pillars.

The Modern City of Ashkelon

In the story of Samson we have already seen that the system of government practiced by the Philistines centered around five major cities, each being ruled by a lord (seren).

This fact of there being five different Philistine capitals also explains what David meant in his elegy when Saul was killed by the Philistines, "Tell it not in Gath, publish it not in the streets of Ashkelon" (2 Sam. 1:20). He was saying that he did not want the Philistines to boast in their capital cities about the death of King Saul of Israel. (Other details of this story are elaborated in Section V dealing with the times of Saul and David.)

This excavation is at modern Ashkelon, one of the five Philistine capitals. David said, "Publish it not in Gath," he meant that Saul's death should not be a point of boasting for the Philistines in their capitals — Ashkelon was one, and Gath was another.

Today Ashkelon is one of the most popular cities of Israel. Its beach is delightful for sun-lovers and swimmers. From an archaeological point of view, there is a park which should be a "must" for visitors to this ancient land. Statues of gods and other figures of ancient times (mainly the Roman period) have been brought together in an impressive display. The ongoing archaeological dig is in an area between the park and the ocean.

Ashkelon — "They Shall Build the Old Waste Places" (Isa. 58:12).

Ashkelon is mentioned as being "carried off" in the famous Egyptian Merneptah Stele dating to about 1230 B.C. In the second century B.C. it gained the protection of the Roman authorities against the Jews, and became a free city. Herod the Great had magnificent structures erected there. It was eventually destroyed by Saladin in A.D. 1191 when Richard the Lionhearted was closing in on the area. Today it is again in the hands of the Israelite people.

Our picture reminds us of the fact that prophecies about Israel continue to be fulfilled. The sign is at Ashkelon, and the Isaiah prophecy looks on to a time when the nation is restored, the yoke is removed from them, and their light will rise in darkness. Spiritually, not all its requirements have been completely fulfilled, but a start has been made. Once again, "coming events are casting their shadows." Thus Ashkelon is typical of the fact that ancient ruins will be rebuilt, age-old foundations will be restored, and streets with dwellings will be restored (Isa. 58: 12).

This sign at modern Ashkelon is a reminder of Isaiah's prophecy that ancient ruins would be rebuilt, age-old foundations restored, and streets re-made with houses for Hebrew people to live in.

Gibeon of Samuel

This is modern Gibeon, the site of the ancient city where Samuel resided. From here he went on circuit as he exercised his judgeship. It was also where (later) Solomon had his wonderful dream and was given the gift of wisdom.

Nevertheless, the Lord raised up judges, which delivered them out of the hand of those that spoiled them (Judg. 2:16).

After the death of Joshua the Children of Israel forsook the Lord, serving the gods of the Canaanites. Despite the repeated periods of backsliding apostasy, God manifested both His grace and the certainty of His original covenant with Abraham by just repeatedly raising up judges to lead the people in revival and restoration. Altogether 13 such judges are named in the Book of Judges, these being Othniel, Ehud, Shamgar, Deborah (with Barak), Gideon, Abimelech, Tola, Jair, Jephthah, Ibzan, Elon, Abdon, and Samson. These were followed by Samuel (Eli was a priest rather than a judge), the last of the judges. Othniel, the first, was of the tribe of Judah, but the others came from a total of at least six other tribes.

Gibeon is where Samuel lived. This is also the city whose inhabitants tricked Joshua and deceived him into signing a peace treaty, as told in Joshua 9. They knew that Joshua's troops were likely to overrun the whole land, because they recognized the power of Jehovah. Although Joshua was deceived into signing the treaty he kept his word, and the city was not destroyed. He even went to their defense when five Canaanite kings attacked them. The people of Gibeon were made to be servants, being especially used in drawing water and cutting wood. Despite its rather easy submission to Joshua (Josh. 9:3), Gibeon was an important and impressive city.

Gibeon was a great city, like one of the royal cities ... and all its men were mighty (Josh. 10:2).

The Wine Vats at Ancient Gibeon

Gibeon became famous for the production and export of choice wines. These round holes in the rock are actually openings to wine cellars dating to about the eighth or seventh century before the birth of Christ. Some 63 of these were found, and each could store 42 jars, with a capacity of 32 liters each. They could be sealed by a capstone fitted over them, and they would maintain a constant temperature of 18°C.

Some of the wine jars have been found with the name of the city, El-Jib, and the producer's name actually stamped on their handles. As a "royal city," presumably its wines graced the tables of kings of Israel from time to time.

It was at this site that Solomon later prepared a great feast, and here he was given a wonderful dream by God with the opportunity to choose what he would. Solomon chose wisdom and knowledge rather than riches and honor, which he could have chosen (2 Chron. 1:3-13).

The Great Pool at Gibeon

This rock-cut pool at Gibeon is a little over six miles (10 km) north of Jerusalem; it is about 35 feet in diameter and 35 feet deep. These ancient people had an excellent water supply inside their fortified city. As well as this great pool, the excavators found a tunnel that led to a spring outside the city, camouflaged to be hidden from the enemy. The spiral staircase was about

five feet wide, and it led to the bottom of the pool where 27 jar handles were discovered. From the inscriptions on the handles both the site (Gibeon) and the names of the pottery merchants were identified.

These were related to the famous wine cellars at this site, these being holes cut into the rock. They could be sealed by a capstone that fitted over the top — and incidentally they could maintain a temperature of 18°C. The cellars would have provided storage for about 25,000 gallons of wine. It seems that the wine from these rock-hewn vats was taken out and poured into smaller jars for sale.

It is worth noticing that the handles had names such as Amariah, Azariah, and Hananiah, these being biblical names, though not necessarily the same characters. However, it is also interesting to realize that Jeremiah referred to Hananiah his opponent as coming from Gibeon (Jer. 28:1).

Right through the Scriptures we are constantly reminded, in direct and indirect ways, that these are historical records about real people who lived against known backgrounds.

Spiral Staircase at Gibeon

This spiral staircase is in the great pool at El-Jib, the ancient Gibeon. Both the pool and the staircase are remarkable engineering achievements. This great rock-cut pool was the scene of an interesting contest, recorded in 2 Samuel 2 of 12 men from the tribe of Benjamin, and 12 who were the servants of David, fighting each other. We read that each of the warriors "thrust his sword in his fellow's side; so they fell down together: wherefore that place was called Helkath-hazzurim, which is in Gibeon" (2 Sam. 2:16;ASV). ("Helkath-hazzurim" means "the field of sword edges.")

The contest was actually arranged by Abner and Joab (2 Sam. 2:13-14). All 24 of the young men died — apparently to save the main body of the troops. There are archaeological records that refer to this practice between opposing armies, and this gruesome story at Gibeon illustrates the factual nature of biblical recording. Although the story is distasteful, it is a record of truth.

The same principle of representatives being chosen to fight is demonstrated in the challenge of the Philistine champion Goliath against Israel, as shown in 1 Samuel 17:9. If their champion won, it was supposed to be evidence of the superiority of their god. This explains why the Philistines fled in disarray when David defeated Goliath.

These stairs lead down the side of the great pool. It was here at a later time that a contest took place when young men were chosen from the two opposing sides of Israel, and they all died as they fought.

A Brief Summary of Section III

The Conquest of Canaan was a real challenge to Joshua, Moses' appointed successor. This man's name was originally Hoshea (Saviour — see Num. 13:10), but it was changed to Je-Hoshea — Joshua, meaning "Jehovah is Salvation."

At the beginning of Joshua we read the Lord's instruction, "Arise, go over this Jordan. . . . Be strong and of good courage. . . . This Book of the Law shall not depart from your mouth" (Josh. 1: 2-8). Throughout his lifetime Joshua followed the written law of Moses and obeyed the instructions of the Lord. Clearly this law was in written form — this Book of the Law.

Joshua opposed the corruption and brutality of the Canaanites, and saw swift victories against Canaanite cities, commencing with Jericho. Those victories are unexplainable apart from the Captain of the host (the Lord himself) going with him (see Josh. 5:14).

Looking at the Ruins of Jericho

A visiting archaeologist is examining the site of ancient Jericho. He is especially noting the areas of burning, shown by the black sections in the balk here pictured.

The People Are Established in the Land

Jericho has come to epitomize differing viewpoints about the date of the Exodus from Egypt and the conquest of Canaan. In the 1930s Dr. John Garstang excavated and suggested a date of about 1400 B.C. for the city's destruction.

In the 1950s Dr. Kathleen Kenyon again excavated, and severely criticized Garstang's conclusions.

More recently there has been a moving back to Garstang at many (not all) points. At face value (based largely on 1 Kings 6:1) the date given by the Bible would seem to be about 1400 B.C. for Jericho's destruction.

Joshua exterminated Canaanites whose "cup of iniquity was full" — a people guilty of child sacrifice, "sacred" prostitution of both sexes, and false assumption of divine powers. He warned the Israelites that they too would know this judgment of God if they departed from His holy standards.

The example and challenge of Joshua was very effective in his lifetime. However, after he died there was no comparable leadership, and time and time again the people fell into idolatry, especially by their worship of the false deities of the Canaanites. Consequently, they fell into the hands of their enemies, but were redeemed when they repented. God sent a series of deliverers ("judges") at those times of repentance.

As the people returned to the Lord, they knew peace. The Book of Judges reminds us of God's faithfulness to His covenant, even with a backsliding, wayward people.

We have not dealt in great depth with the archaeological conclusions that relate to the Book of Judges. One reason is that archaeologists have had serious differences within their own ranks, especially as to dating the cities that have been excavated.

The last decade has seen bitter controversy and criticism, especially centering around the date of the Exodus. The researches of Dr. Bryan Wood have been one of the effective results to show that Jericho fell to Joshua about 1440 B.C., and it is one reason why some leaders have "gone silent" or have gone more public with the suggestion, "There never was an Exodus."

Despite the problems dating particular sites, "Judges" is an important link between Joshua as Moses' successor, and the circumstances leading to kingship in Israel. There were several pointers to kingship, including shared language, religion, and historical background. These people were still the seed of Abraham, and enjoyed the privilege of a special covenant relationship with Jehovah.

Despite many critical attacks (e.g. — as we have stated — in regard to the destruction of Jericho) there is no properly established archaeological fact relating to the times of Joshua and the judges that shows the Bible to be in historical error. In fact, modern research continues to demonstrate the historical integrity and accuracy of the writers in ways that point on (and back) to Psalm 119:89:

Forever, O Lord, thy word is settled in heaven.

That, in fact, is the consistent pattern for both Old and New Testaments.

SECTION IV

A GREATER-THAN-JOSHUA IS HERE

For if Joshua had given them rest, then he would not afterwards
have spoken of another day (Heb. 4:8).

On the road to Emmaus Jesus had shown himself to be enshrined in the Books of Moses, "in all the Prophets," and "in all the Scriptures." (Luke 24:27) In this section we consider One who is foreshadowed in the life of Joshua, even our Lord who is greater than that great military leader Joshua.

Thus, in Joshua God is seen in history, ever in control of the affairs of men. His ways make known His character and His will for man. As they honor and obey Him, blessing follows. If they dishonor Him, judgment will eventually fall.

Joshua had been one of the two faithful spies when he and Caleb said they could prevail against the Canaanites in the strength of the Lord, even though the other ten spies said they could not because of the giants in the land. It is little wonder that this man of faith and courage was appointed as successor to Moses, and we are not surprised to see the divine seal upon the appointment.

But a greater-than-Joshua is here, for our Lord not only came against mortal giants but against the rulers of darkness — against the one who had set himself up as god of the world. Our Lord is the author and finisher of our faith. He was engaged in greater battle than Joshua ever experienced, and His victory is far more complete. A greater-than-Joshua is here.

When Joshua was commissioned by the Lord the River Jordan was overflowing its banks (Josh. 3). It was the time of harvest. These people had no experience with boats, for they had spent a lifetime in the desert, so they had to trust God to enable them to cross that river. God answered their faith. Joshua obeyed the Lord, and they went down to the river expecting God to do the impossible, and He did. Joshua's wonderful faith was vindicated, for the children of Israel were able to cross that river on dry ground.

The Lord Our Salvation

Joshua's name originally was Hoshea, which means salvation, but an abbreviated form of the name of Jehovah was added and his name became Je-Hoshea, or Joshua (Num. 13:16), which means "the Lord is Saviour." This Hebrew name is the same as Jesus in the Greek, and in this way Joshua was a very wonderful pointer to the heavenly Jesus, the One of whom it was said: "(Mary) shall bring forth a Son, and you shall call His name Jesus, for He will save His people from their sins" (Matt. 1:21).

Just as Joshua was the successor to Moses and had the privilege of leading the children of Israel into the land, so the Lord Jesus Christ is the One who took away the penalty of the Law and gave us the right to enter the heavenly land. Now we can say with the apostle Paul in the Epistle to the Ephesians, "God . . . made us sit together in the heavenly places in Christ Jesus" (Eph. 2:4-6).

In passing, it should be mentioned that the Epistle to the Ephesians is the New Testament counterpart to the Old Testament Book of Joshua. In Joshua they entered Canaan; in Ephesians we enter the heavenlies. Our heavenly Joshua has conquered, conquered where the Law could not. Christ has brought us into the very presence of God and has given us a rest which is eternal; Joshua's "rest" was incomplete and temporary.

Crossing the River of Death

There is much typological teaching in the Book of Joshua, and one lesson is in chapter 3 where we see that Joshua and the children of Israel crossed the River Jordan. The River Jordan had to be crossed so that the Promised Land could be entered, and a way had to be opened miraculously. Spiritually, that illustrates our entrance into the heavenly land. The river of death was crossed by our heavenly Joshua, and now we, too, have a miraculous entry into the eternal inheritance.

The priests went ahead of the people, carrying the ark of the covenant. The ark was itself a symbol of Christ, and as we watch those priests waiting in the middle of the opened Jordan until all the people pass over, we see another lovely illustration of the work of Christ. Our Lord is our great High Priest, the One who has offered himself on our behalf to God. Every child of God who comes to the Christ of Calvary for salvation is met by the Lord in the very center of the river of death. The Son of God is infinite, and it is just as though He died separately for every individual who accepts Him as substitute. "The wages of sin is death, but the gift of God is eternal life" (Rom. 6:23). He took our penalty on himself.

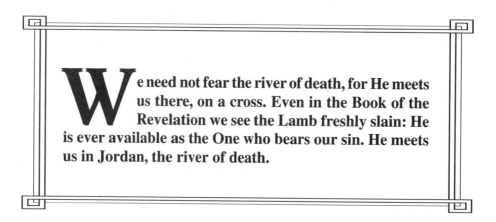

We need not fear the river of death, for He meets us there, on a cross. Even in the Book of the Revelation we see the Lamb freshly slain: He is ever available as the One who bears our sin. He meets us in Jordan, the river of death.

Another application is that as we pass on from this life, then, too, He meets us. The Psalmist wrote long ago, "Yea, though I walk through the valley of the shadow of death, I will fear no evil; For You are with me." As our Lord told His disciples, "I am with you, to the end of the age." So death holds no undue fear for the Christian, for in a special sense at that time the Lord meets him and escorts him over the river of death, into the heavenly land of promise.

Another similarity to the life of Christ can be seen in the erection of the memorial pillars which commemorated the crossing of the Jordan. Our Lord also instituted a memorial to commemorate His crossing the river of death on our behalf. The bread and the wine continually point back as a memorial of Calvary. They are our memorial pillars. They remind us that we have been carried over the river of death.

Joshua Meets the Captain of the Lord's Host

Before the Israelites attacked Jericho, Joshua found himself face to face with the angel of the Lord, and Joshua dared to challenge this One before he realized it was the Lord himself.

In an earlier study we have seen that occasionally our Lord revealed himself in Old Testament times in the form of a Man, in a series of visitations known as Christophanies. This is one such appearance, and as Joshua challenged this One who called himself "the Captain of the host of the Lord" Joshua was told, "Take your sandal off your foot, for the place where you stand is holy" (Josh. 5:15).

Joshua fell on his face and worshipped this One and NO man or angel should dare take to himself worship: this was the Son of God himself. Just as Moses had to remove his shoes in the presence of the Lord on Mount Sinai, so now Joshua had the same experience in the presence of the Lord before the attack against Jericho.

At this time Joshua learned that the Lord himself would be in the midst, with His sword drawn on behalf of His chosen people. His presence would not always be visible, but that did not make it any less real. They were to meet spiritual as well as physical enemies, but the Captain of the host was with them, His sword drawn, ready to fight for His people. Probably there were many times when Joshua needed a fresh reminder of that wonderful experience, for Joshua was but a man, liable to doubts and failure, but his faith was ever real.

This is seen symbolically when we first read of Joshua in the time of Moses. Joshua took a leading part in the battle against Amalek, who is seen by many commentators as speaking of the flesh. Joshua showed a spiritual pattern in that great contest, recorded in Exodus 17:8-16.

Joshua teaches us the lesson that we need deliverance from the flesh, our Amalek, and that we have a mighty deliverer, even our heavenly Joshua, the Lord Jesus Christ. He is the Captain of the host. Our Lord could say to those early disciples, "I am with you to the end of the age." This seemed to be a paradox for He also told them He was about to leave them. But though He was about to leave them, yet He would send the comforter, the Holy Spirit, One whose being was as His own. Now, spiritually, we inherit the promise, "Lo I am with you always, even to the end of the age."

As we, like Joshua, meet spiritual enemies, the Lord goes before us. He knows our frame that we are but dust, so He is ever ready to heed our cry and to supply our need, whatever it might be.

Seeing the Walls of Jericho Collapse

Joshua saw the walls of Jericho collapse when he put the commandment of God to the test, and his faith was vindicated.

Jericho is often seen as a picture of the world in the grip of the enemy of the people of God. The name Jericho itself points to moon worship, and there is much false worship in the world today. Just as surely as Joshua and the warriors of Israel were challenged to defeat that city by trusting the living God, so surely does our heavenly Joshua lead us against the forces of evil today. In His strength the walls of Jericho can still collapse — not the physical walls of course, but the barriers which have been raised by the enemy in an attempt to prevent "the entrance of Your words gives light" (Ps. 119:130). Our Lord said, "All authority has been given to Me." (Matt. 28:18) Even the gates of Hades cannot stand against Him.

A greater-than-Joshua is here, for as we go to the Epistle to the Hebrews we are reminded that Joshua could not give the children of Israel permanent rest. Joshua gave them temporary victories, and it was a wonderful series of victories that he did give them. Nevertheless those victories lasted only during his lifetime. As soon as he died there was a great declension.

Joshua could give rest only while he himself was there, but the Lord Jesus Christ, our heavenly Joshua, has given us a victory that is permanent, for He is ever with us. He gives a rest that is eternal, having forever set to flight the forces of the enemy. The captain of our salvation leads us into our heavenly possession where we are seated with Him. The victory is won, though there will be testings until the ultimate victory is final and eternal. Truly, a greater-than-Joshua is here.

Joshua led the children of Israel in their great conquest of the land of Canaan. There were seven victories in seven years, which is a remarkable contrast with the seven apostasies, the seven oppressions, and the seven times when divine deliverance was needed in the years following his death. But a greater-than-Joshua is here, even the Lord Jesus Christ who fought the great battle of Calvary, and then "sat down," His victory completed, knowing that henceforth His enemies would be as His footstool. Unlike Joshua, our heavenly deliverer did not lose His power because He died.

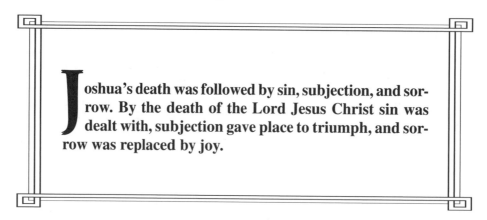

Joshua's death was followed by sin, subjection, and sorrow. By the death of the Lord Jesus Christ sin was dealt with, subjection gave place to triumph, and sorrow was replaced by joy.

Joshua's work was finished at his death, but Jesus died and rose again, and His work continues through you and me. A greater-than-Joshua is here.

"As for Me and My House, We Will Serve the Lord"

Perhaps one of the most important incidents in the life of Joshua is that famous charge to the children of Israel:

> Now therefore, fear the Lord, serve Him in sincerity and in truth, and put away the gods which your fathers served on the other side of the River [= Euphrates] and in Egypt. Serve the Lord! And if it seem evil to you to serve the Lord, choose for yourselves this day whom you will serve, whether the gods which your fathers served that were on the other side of the River, or the gods of the Amorites, in whose land you dwell. But as for me and my house, we will serve the Lord.
>
> So the people answered and said: "Far be it from us that we should forsake the Lord to serve other gods" (Josh. 24:14-16).

It was at this time the people declared that they would serve the true God, "for the Lord our God is He . . . who did those great signs in our sight" (Josh. 24:17).

Joshua was suggesting a choice to the people: if they would not serve Jehovah, they should choose to serve either the gods "beyond the river," or the gods of the Canaanites in whose land they were now dwelling. He made it clear that he would serve none of those gods, but would in fact serve Jehovah. As far as Joshua was concerned, a greater-than-the-gods-of-the-Canaanites was here, even the true God Jehovah.

Before we consider the gods of the land, we shall briefly ask ourselves what Joshua meant when he referred to the "gods beyond the river," for they were the first alternative put before the people.

The Gods of Abraham's Ancestors

The word "river" is actually translated "flood" in the Authorized Version, but the meaning is actually "river." That river was the River Euphrates. There is a very great contrast between the false worship associated with the moon god at Ur (at that time on the Euphrates River) and Haran, and the way of life and worship of the followers of Jehovah, the true God of Israel. All sorts of abominable practices were carried on in the name of Nanna the moon god, not the least repugnant being those associated with sex.

In another of these present series we have seen that not only were there women priestesses who were literally sacred prostitutes, but the practice was that other women devotees should also offer themselves at least once at the temple. The theory was that by doing this they were sacrificing themselves to the gods. It is little wonder that the excavator — Sir Leonard Woolley — reported that the real blot on this ancient Sumerian culture was the degradation of the womenfolk.

That was not all. In the New Testament, in Romans 1, we read of men who turned from women, burning in their lust towards each other, and eventually God gave them up because of their wickedness. At Ur, the city from which Abraham departed, some "priests" took office in the temple as sacred sodomites. This was not just a private act, but was an actual office, being part of the ritualism associated with the worship of the moon god Nanna.

Abraham left it all, for he knew that his God was a Holy God. Clearly, the concept of God in the Bible is greatly superior to the ideas other ancient peoples had about their gods.

The holiness associated with the worship of Jehovah was unknown to other peoples. It is no wonder that we read in Acts 7:2, "The God of glory appeared to our father Abraham when he was in Mesopotamia, before he dwelt in Haran," and the message goes on to declare how God called Abraham out from that land into a new land that would be shown to Abraham.

We are again reminded of that as we see Joshua challenging the people. In worshipping the gods "beyond the river" they would have been going back spiritually, rejecting their covenant relationship with God which had been established through Abraham. That covenant included a call to leave the land beyond the river, with all its repugnant polytheistic worship.

On the other hand, Joshua also threw out a challenge to the people to reject the worship of gods in the land where they were now dwelling. These people did have highly developed religious systems, and excavations (e.g., at Ras Shamra in Northern Syria) have silenced many critical arguments against the possibility of the highly developed religious ceremonial system of the Book of Leviticus. Canaanite rituals were advanced, and so they showed that the Israelites also could have utilized such practices, but there were also essential differences from the religious practices of "the chosen people."

Canaanite Abominations

Canaanite rituals offered dangerous similarities to the Hebrew religion. They were only surface similarities, but to those who wanted a form of godliness without the holy living demanded of His people by the Hebrew God, Canaanite religion was a dangerous alternative. Many Israelites did accept the worship of Baal rather than that of the true God. Famous ancient fragments of potsherds known as the Samaria Ostraca make it clear that the name of Baal was common as a personal name among the Hebrew people.

Human sacrifices were relatively commonplace in Canaanite religion, and funerary jars have been found with the skeletons of little children who had suffocated after being buried alive in the foundation pillars of temples and other buildings.

Another relevant aspect relating to Canaanite religion is that when the Israelites departed from the Lord they would make images of Baal or Asherah, but never of Jehovah. No certain image of Jehovah has ever been found in Israelite civilizations, though figures of Baal have been recovered. In the Decalogue, the Ten Commandments, they were enjoined to make no images of Jehovah, and so deeply was this ingrained that even if they did turn away and make images of gods, they would not make them of the true

God with whom they as a people were in covenant relationship.

Even in this there was a deeply ingrained knowledge of the fact that a greater-than-all-gods was here, even Jehovah the true God who had made himself known to men. Thus, even in their backslidings, the people of Israel were acknowledging that a greater-than-all-the-gods was here. It was Jethro the priest of Midian who made the statement as it is recorded in Exodus, and the people themselves acknowledged its truth even as they made images of Baal, or of Asherah, but never of Jehovah.

Through their history the Israelites were constantly challenged to depart from the false worship that surrounded them. In Joshua's day the people were greatly influenced by Joshua's example and by his constant giving of himself in their service. The Lord Jesus said of himself, "I am among you as One who serves." His self-giving was entire — even to death. In His resurrection life He still serves others through those who accept His challenge to "Come, follow."

Here in our pilgrimage we have the privilege of going with Him, of rejecting the idols in our surroundings, of saying "No" to the possibilities of any other way of life, and of saying with the children of Israel to Joshua, "We will serve the Lord!" For a greater-than-Joshua is here.

Joshua and the Book of the Law

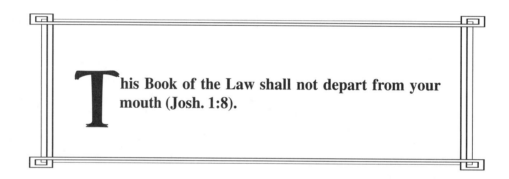

This Book of the Law shall not depart from your mouth (Josh. 1:8).

Joshua was one of the great men of Scripture, and the first chapter of the book that bears his name wonderfully tells of his character. We listen as the Lord says to Joshua, "Moses My servant is dead. Now therefore, arise, go over this Jordan, you and all this people . . . children of Israel" (Josh. 1:2). The Lord told Joshua to be strong and of good courage, and He himself would be with Him as his guide. As we go on through the record we learn that Joshua was a mighty man of faith.

Joshua was the appointed successor to Moses, and is a wonderful type of the Lord Jesus Christ. Scripture says that the Law came by Moses, but grace and truth came by Jesus Christ. The Law could not bring us back to God, for it only told where we failed and pointed to our spiritual death and separation from God.

It needed a greater power than the Law to bring us to God, even Jesus Christ who took the curse of the Law and became sin for us. He died in our place, as our substitute. As Moses is a reminder of the Law and its penalty of death, so Joshua reminds us of a new victory as we enter our inheritance.

Joshua was intimately associated with Moses in the giving of the Law in that he was part of the way up the mountain of Sinai when the Decalogue (the Ten Commandments) was given, and he attended Moses at the gate of the tent of meeting. He is referred to as Moses' servant and as his loyal assistant. (Exod. 24:13, 32:15-17, 33:11; Num. 11:28.)

Our heavenly Joshua (Jesus) became subject to the Law, and as the servant of Jehovah He was the only Man ever to keep perfectly the law of God. A greater-than-Joshua was here.

When the Lord commissioned Joshua, among other things we notice the command, "This Book of the Law shall not depart from your mouth, but you shall meditate in it day and night" (Josh. 1:8). In this part of God's Word we are referred to a "Book of the Law." When we go to Hebrews we find that it is quite clearly not just any book of the law, but "THIS Book of the Law." When we read the command of Moses in Deuteronomy 31:26, we find it is just as definite. There is an established Book of the Law. In Deuteronomy Moses gave instructions for the Book of the Law to be placed alongside the ark of the covenant as a witness against the people.

Perhaps to complete the picture we should move ahead to 2 Kings 22:8 where we read:

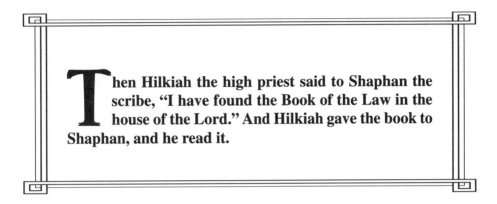

Then Hilkiah the high priest said to Shaphan the scribe, "I have found the Book of the Law in the house of the Lord." And Hilkiah gave the book to Shaphan, and he read it.

This last verse is the basis of a major critical argument — that the book which was found in 621 B.C., in the reign of Josiah, had been written only within that generation, and was in fact a pious fraud being foisted on a credulous people. Let us simply say that it is much easier, and ultimately far more satisfying, to accept the biblical statements at face value. The argument against there being a Book of the Law in the days of Moses and Joshua originally stemmed from such ideas as there being no method of writing in those days. While those views have been modified — for in fact they have been shown to be ridiculous — much of the critical opposition to the genuineness of the Mosaic source documents has continued. The only reasonable alternative, ultimately, is to accept the integrity of the written records as such.

Joshua was told to meditate in this Book of the Law day and night. This Law witnessed to God's perfect standards, and it was also a witness against the people when they failed to reach those standards. Even the devout Joshua was capable of failure. We see his tendency to blame the Lord for the defeat of his troops at Ai (Josh. 7:6-9), and also his failure to exalt the Lord at a time when he wrongly entered into a league with the people of Gibeon — he did not seek the mind of the Lord (Josh. 9:14).

When we study the life of Christ we "find no fault in this Man," even as Pilate said at His trial. Our Lord himself could ask, "Which of you convicts Me of sin?" (John 8:46), and no one could. He is the only Man who could say, "I delight to do Your will, O My God," all the days of His life, the only One who could perfectly, and always, say, "I have glorified You on the earth."

Our Lord commended the law of Moses, and as we go through His teaching we find that He specifically endorsed all of the Commandments except that one relating to the keeping of the Sabbath Day. He himself said of the Sabbath, "My Father has been working until now, and I have been working" (John 5:17).

We who are believers in Jesus Christ have entered into a new rest, where His new work is His new creation. And now, after His new work, He has risen from the dead, and we remember the first day of the week as the special day associated with that new creation. This day is referred to in Revelation 1:10, known in early Church history as "The Lord's Day" — the first day which was kept with gladness.

Our Lord witnessed to the authority of the law of Moses, and yet He showed that He himself was beyond that Law. In the Sermon on the Mount (Matthew chapters 5 to 7) He could refer to various aspects of the law of Moses and then go on to say, "But I say to you." He would go beyond the act to the motive itself. The look of lust was in the same class as the act of adultery; unwarranted anger came from the same root as murder.

As we look again at this command to Joshua, we see a great similarity to our Lord. Joshua was told "This Book of the Law shall not depart from your mouth, but you shall meditate in it day and night, that you may observe to do according to all that is written in it. For then you will make your way prosperous, and then you will have good success" (Josh. 1:8).

Who more than our Lord meditated in the Book of the Law? Who more than He observed to do what was written therein? The Scriptures were His delight, and it is a wonderful study to see the ways in which the Lord Jesus Christ meditated in them, and through them the path of divine choice was confirmed to Him.

Scripture Cannot Be Broken!

When He was tempted in the wilderness, our Lord resisted the devil by references to the writings of Deuteronomy, as three times He declared, "It is written. . . . It is written. . . . It is written." (Matthew 4:4, 7, 10).

In Mark 12:24 he told His critics that they did not know the Scriptures or the power of God. Clearly, to our Lord the words of Scripture were, in fact, the words of God, even when this meant a recognition of the suffering which was to be His by divine appointment. An illustration of this is in Matthew 26:31: "Then Jesus said to them, All of you will be made to stumble because of Me this night, FOR IT IS WRITTEN, "I will strike the Shepherd, And the sheep of the flock will be scattered" (emphasis added).

Any doubt as to our Lord's constant meditation upon the Scriptures must be put aside when we come to Luke 2:47 and read of the 12-year-old Son of Mary who could amaze the temple doctors by His understanding and answers. He was, of course, the Son of God with a knowledge beyond that of any other human being, but it is also true that "Jesus increased in wisdom and stature, and in favor with God and men" (Luke 2:52). It is not possible to decide at what point or in what ways the divine and human were separated, for in this Man, Jesus of Nazareth, dwelt all the fullness of the godhead bodily (Col. 2:9). He was truly God and truly Man, and yet He knew what it was to meditate in the Scriptures and to see in them the revelation of himself as the Saviour of those who would come to Him. After His resurrection we read, "And beginning at Moses and all the prophets, He expounded to them in all the Scriptures the things concerning himself" (Luke 24:27).

There are many other ways in which we could develop this subject of our Lord meditating in the Scriptures and observing all that was written therein. A greater-than-Joshua is here, for, as we have already said, at no point could the finger of criticism be justly leveled at this One who so completely fulfilled the law of God.

A Voice ... and the Word

Joshua was but a voice whose sound would linger for a moment, and then only be known in the memory of his people and honored by posterity. He is rightly remembered as one of the greatest men in all the history of Israel, and he was a worthy successor to the great man Moses with whom God would speak so personally on that special mountaintop. He was responsible for the nation recognizing the need to follow Jehovah, even as they had been so faithfully taught in the days of Moses as leader. When Joshua died there was serious decline, and the Book of Judges tells us of a need of a whole series of leaders to be raised up. The importance of Joshua can hardly be over-estimated, but for all that when compared with our Lord, Joshua was but a passing voice, as we have already stated.

The Lord Jesus Christ was more than a passing voice. In His lifetime people marveled at the gracious words that proceeded out of His mouth, and that is not surprising, for this One was the very Word of God, the One greater than Moses and greater than Joshua, because He is himself the image of the Invisible God. Joshua could meditate in that Law and marvel at the wisdom of the great God who therein revealed himself. The Lord Jesus Christ was himself the Word who is made unto us wisdom, righteousness and sanctification.

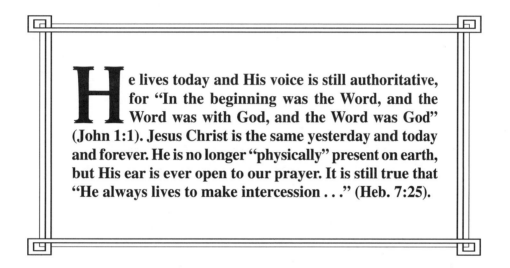

He lives today and His voice is still authoritative, for "In the beginning was the Word, and the Word was with God, and the Word was God" (John 1:1). Jesus Christ is the same yesterday and today and forever. He is no longer "physically" present on earth, but His ear is ever open to our prayer. It is still true that "He always lives to make intercession . . ." (Heb. 7:25).

We have referred to the series of defeats after Joshua's death, and as we begin to study the Book of Judges we learn of the decline now that the strong leader has departed. It was not really until the leadership of Samuel that spiritual strength was again established. He was born in answer to his mother's prayers, and was given to the Lord before he was born (1 Sam. 1:9-11). He was trained for the service of the Lord from his early childhood (1 Sam. 1:24-28), and he faithfully served Him from childhood to the end of his life (1 Sam. 2:18, 3:1-21, 12:1-5).

Once again there was strong spiritual leadership and the people prospered, as they prospered in the days of Joshua's strong spiritual leadership. However, all men such as Joshua and Samuel die, or become too old to continue their best work. In contrast to that, our heavenly Joshua lives forever, and we who follow Him rest in the certain knowledge of His final victory.

As we close, we reflect on the verse at the beginning of the chapter, Hebrews 4:8, which indicates that Joshua could not give the people permanent rest. Contrast that with our heavenly Joshua: Jesus died, but He lived again. He can never become old, for He is the Eternal One, and He gives a rest that is eternal.

Truly, a greater-than-Joshua (and a greater-than-Samuel) is here.

SECTION V

SAUL AND DAVID IN THE LIGHT OF HISTORY

The Valley of Elah

This is the general area where the Philistines challenged the Israelites in the time of the giant Goliath. At that time the young stripling David was prepared to go against Goliath, stating that he came in the name of the Lord of hosts.

Towards the end of the Judges period, the Israelites demanded a king "to judge us like all the nations" (1 Sam. 8:5), and Saul the son of Kish was eventually so anointed. He had much trouble with the Philistines, and the Bible especially tells of the taunting by the giant Goliath. Dr. Edward Hindsen has a highly relevant comment about the contest between David and Goliath in *The Philistines in the Old Testament*:

> Goliath challenged the armies of Israel to select a champion from their ranks to confront him in a battle of championship. The single combatants would decide the fate of each army. The individual victor would bring victory to his army, and the loser would cause his people to go into slavery. He defied Israel to "send forth her man," but all Israel was afraid. If anyone was to answer this challenge it should have been newly-elected King Saul, the leader of Israel who stood head and shoulders above any man in Israel (1 Sam. 9:2).
>
> The concept of victory by championship battle is definitely Aegean and again substantiates the origin of the Philistines. Achilles and Hector fought in such contest in Homeric

legends. Livy tells of the champions of the Loratii and the Curiatii. Parallels may also be found among the Hittites of Asia Minor, the same area later occupied by the Trojans. The Hittites had teams of champions similar to David's 12 men of 2 Samuel 2:12.[22]

David Picked Five Stones from the Stream

David would not go in Saul's armor . . . but he took five stones from the brook in the Elah Valley. Only one was needed, and the giant Goliath was entirely without power. David came in the name of the Lord of hosts. Dr. Hindsen further states:

David's contest with Goliath was meant to be a demonstration of the power of the Philistine gods. It was a disastrous failure for the Philistines. David's God Jehovah was the true God!

The concept of such a battle was based upon the Philistine concept of religion. They believed in the power of all gods to choose to aid the armies of men . . . to the Philistines a battle of champions would test the favor of the gods. If the gods could give the champion victory, they could give the entire army victory. Therefore, the test of the conflict was a test of the power of the gods. This explains why Goliath made a mockery of the gods of the Israelites. (v. 45) If He could not empower their champion, how could He give victory to their nation.[23]

That is the background to David declaring that he came in the name of the Lord of hosts. As we are reminded in this picture of the stream in the Valley of Elah, David simply chose five stones from the river bed in this area (the course of such a stream would change from time to time). Only one stone was needed. With his sling he cast his first stone, it entered the forehead of Goliath, and the victory was the Lord's. David gave all the honor to the true God of war, Jehovah. He was the God who controlled the affairs of men, no matter what their boasting giants might declare.

Bethlehem of Judah

Now it came to pass, in the days when the judges ruled, that there was a famine in the land. And a certain man of Bethlehem, Judah, went to dwell in the country of Moab, he and his wife and his two sons. The name of the man was Elimelech, the name of his wife was Naomi, and the name of his two sons were Mahlon and Chilion — Ephrathites of Bethlehem, Judah (Ruth 1:1-2).

The Countryside from Bethlehem Today

Ruth was associated with Bethlehem, for in this general area Ruth the Moabitess was allowed to glean in the fields of Boaz, a kinsman of her late husband. She was the great-grandmother of David, Israel's king — a man after God's own heart.

These introductory verses, as well as the closing genealogy (Ruth 4:17-22), indicate that the Book of Ruth was written after "the days when the judges ruled." Judges had been replaced by the monarchy. Possibly Samuel in the days of Saul, or even David (Ruth's great-grandson who probably heard the story from his parents) may have written it. Ruth's husband was Boaz, evidently the son of Rahab (Matt. 1:5), the converted harlot (innkeeper?) who joined the Israelites at the fall of Jericho. The story of Ruth, therefore, probably took place during the early part of the judges period, but being written up some time later.

Saul's Fortress at Gibeah

Professor W.F. Albright excavated at Gibeah and found seven occupational levels dating from about 1100 B.C. to 70 A.D. Among those levels were the ashes and charred ruins of an Israelite town that had been burned about the 12th century B.C., apparently the destruction referred to in Judges 19 and 20.

Gibeah Today

This is the site of Saul's ancient fortress at Gibeah, just a few miles north of Jerusalem. The unfinished palace of Jordan's King Hussein is on the site: there would be Arab opposition to either destroying it or re-using it for somebody else.

Today the unfinished palace of King Hussein of Jordan stands at the top of the site (on the West Bank of Israel). Nobody dares take over the building!

Of special interest for the times of Saul was the excavation of a two-story fortress, measuring about 155 x 170 feet. The stone walls were hammer dressed and they averaged between 8 and 10 feet thick, with a stone staircase which led to the second floor. It is thought that one of the rooms found here was the audience room where the young David played his harp when Saul needed to be soothed — it was a room measuring 14 x 23 feet. In the ruins dating to this period cooking pots were found, together with grinding stones and spinning whorls and even a gaming board. Large quantities of food were also found. It was blackened, partly as a result of exposure over the centuries.

Philistine Anthropoid Coffin Found at Beth-shean

This coffin found at Beth-shean is a reminder that Philistines were in the area at the time of David and Saul. The Philistines killed Saul and his three sons on Mount Gilboa and then took their bodies across the plain to Beth-shean. Professor G. Ernest Wright, at that time Professor of Semitics and Old Testament Studies at Harvard University, wrote an article, "Philistine Coffins and Mercenaries" in *The Biblical Archaeologist*, suggesting that the word that the Hebrew people used for "Philistine" meant all "sea peoples." They were the most dominant group in Palestine at the time. This would mean that the earlier reference to "Philistines being in the land in the days of Abraham" would be perfectly acceptable — many critics claimed that this was an anachronism, something written up at a later time. In his book, *The Philistines in the Old Testament*, Dr. Edward E. Hindsen states concerning the Philistines:

> Most historians agree that they came from the eastern Mediterranean area, but their original homeland and migration route are uncertain. It is quite probable that they stopped at Crete, called Caphtor in the Old Testament (Jer. 47:4; Amos 9:7). Also the term *kerethi* ("Cretans") is used in Ezekiel 25:16, Zephaniah 2:5, and 1 Samuel 30:14 to designate the Philistines.[24]

The Gateway at the Entrance to Beth-shean

> Now when the inhabitants of Jabesh Gilead heard of that which the Philistines had done to Saul, all the valiant men arose, and traveled all night, and took the body of Saul and the bodies of his sons from the wall of Beth Shan; and they came to Jabesh, and buried them there. Then they took their bones and buried them under the tamarisk tree at Jabesh, and fasted seven days (1 Sam. 31:11-12).

(The biblical Beth Shan is known today as Beth-shean.)

Gate at Beth-shean

Having climbed the tell from the Roman site, we are on the far left of the Beth-shean mound as it would be seen from the Roman city. It is the area of the gate into the city. It was here that the headless body of Saul would have been placed, along with the bodies of his sons. Saul's head was put inside the Philistine temple on this level and his armor in the Canaanite temple. Men of Jabesh Gilead undertook a forced march to recover the bodies.

There were those who greatly appreciated the activities of their King Saul, especially when he stood by the men of Jabesh Gilead.

Beth-shean — Then and Now

The modern spelling of the biblical Beth-shan is Beth-shean. Beth-shean is an impressive tell — an artificial hill that rose level by level through the centuries. As with many other ancient cities, eventually it became too elevated for easy access, and it was abandoned in favor of a new site on the plain area close by.

The ancient tell is in the background, while the ruins of various Roman buildings can be seen in the foreground. These have been excavated in recent years, especially the 1980s. The excavation continues in the 1990s. Beth-shean has become one of the most impressive tourist attractions in all of Israel because of the finding of extensive Roman remains, including a magnificent amphitheater.

When one sees how close some of these structures in Israel are to the surface, it is somewhat surprising that many more sites have not been carefully excavated in the centuries since Roman times. Records from the past are likely to be increasingly recovered, provided funds are available for excavation. Only a fraction of the ancient cities of Israel have been uncovered.

Here is another view of Beth-shean. The bodies of King Saul and three of his sons were carried by the Philistines across the plain from the mountains of Gilboa behind the tell.

The Death of King Saul

Saul was killed in a battle against the Philistines at Mount Gilboa, in the far background of this picture. The story is told in the Bible in 1 Samuel 31. We read that the men of Israel fled before the Philistines, and among those slain were Saul, Jonathan, and two other sons of Saul. Saul was badly wounded by the arrows of the Philistine archers, and then he fell on his own sword to avoid any further humiliation at the hands of the enemy (1 Sam. 31:4). While he was lying mortally wounded he called on a passing Amalekite young man to "finish him off," and the young man complied with Saul's dying wish (2 Sam. 1:6-16).

Saul's body was carried across the plain and deposited at Beth-shean, the tell (mound) at the center left of this picture. The city of Roman times with its impressive theater is in the foreground.

Centuries of history were covered by the accretions of time until the archaeologists of the 20th century came along and began systematically to uncover the ruins of this famous site of Beth-shean.

Area of Temples at Beth-shean

Critics used to say that the Bible was wrong when it talked about two temples at Beth-shean. The point was made that Philistines and Canaanites were enemy people, and therefore there would not be two separate temples on the one level of Beth-shean.

The Australian archaeologist Allan Rowe (and others) showed in the 1920s and 1930s that there were

On the Top of Beth-shean

Here two temples stood at the level of Beth-shean that corresponded to the times of Saul and David. Critics said there could not be a Canaanite and a Philistine temple at the same level because the two peoples were enemies. The critics were wrong.

indeed two temples, and that they were connected by a corridor-like structure. The critics were wrong. The Philistines had conquered the Canaanites and, rather than offend their gods, they had absorbed them into their own pantheon.

This illustrates an important truth. Very often it has seemed to scholars that the Bible was wrong at particular points, but it almost seems that God takes delight in vindicating His Word. Psalm 119:89 says, "Forever, O Lord, Your word is settled in heaven." The finding of the two temples at Beth-shean was yet another illustration of the continuing fact that "the Bible was right after all."

Two Temples at Beth-shean

So it happened the next day, when the Philistines came to strip the slain, that they found Saul and his three sons fallen on Mount Gilboa. And they cut off his head, and stripped off his armor, and sent word throughout the land of the Philistines, to proclaim it in the temple of their idols and among the people. Then they put his armor in the temple of the Ashtaroths, and they fastened his body to the wall of Beth Shan (1 Sam. 31:8-10).

Australian excavator Allan Rowe found evidence of these two temples when he excavated the tell in the 1930s.

The Temple Area on Beth-shean

Dr. Lawrence T. Geraty is standing in the general area of the Philistine and Canaanite temples referred to in 1 Samuel. The Philistines conquered the Canaanites and took over their pantheon (their collection of gods). The local color of the Bible story is remarkably accurate.

Pottery from Ras Shamra

This pottery came from one of the most important excavations ever — at modern Ras Shamra (the ancient Ugarit) in Syria. Even more important was a large number of clay tablets which threw much light on early Canaanite life. Many of the thousands of tablets touched both economic and religious aspects of life. They effectively silenced the criticism that David's psalms should in the main be attributed to the Maccabean period, 800 years after his time.

This pottery from Ras Shamra is of great interest archaeologically. Ras Shamra was the ancient Ugarit and thousands of tablets were recovered, as well as beautiful pottery showing the magnificence of some aspects of Canaanite culture.

Professor W.F. Albright was arguably one of the greatest archaeologists of all time. In his *History, Archaeology and Christian Humanism* he refers to the fact that "there are still many who hold a Maccabean date for some of the Psalms." He discusses the great relevance of the Ugarit findings, and shows that in the Hebrew biblical text there are many reflections of archaic use. He then writes:

> There can be little doubt, in my opinion, that there are scores of Psalms whose composition may best be dated in the 10th century or shortly afterwards, and it becomes hypercritical to reject the tradition of Davidic sponsorship (which was tantamount to authorship at that earlier period) of a substantial nucleus of the present Book of Psalms. . . . To attribute such Psalms to the Maccabean period is absurd.[25]

Alphabet Script from Ugarit

This is a clay tablet of 30 letters from Ugarit in Syria — believed to be the first alphabetic script yet known to man. It is shown alongside the Canaanite god Baal who was prominent in the writings of Ugarit.

Thousands of documents were found at Ugarit (the modern Ras Shamra). As a result of the findings scholarly criticism against the authenticity (especially dating) of the psalms of David has been refuted. We have already seen that they demonstrated that David's psalms could indeed have been written against the backgrounds claimed for them. At times he even used words and phrases from Canaanite psalms.

One example is related to his eulogy at the time of the death of King Saul. He declared,

> O mountains of Gilboa,
> Let there be no dew nor rain upon you, Nor fields of offerings (2 Sam. 1:21).

The translators did not know what to do with that expression "fields of offerings," but a similar Canaanite expression is "upsurgings of the deep." It appears that David was praying that there would be no dew, no rain, and no water being fed from springs beneath the earth — thus "upsurgings" makes much better sense than "fields of offerings."

The Harp Sounds in Jerusalem Again

This is Shoshanna Harrari. She and her husband, Micah, have come to Israel as Jewish people, returning to their Jewish homeland from the United States. They have established a business in Jerusalem for the making and selling of harps. By careful research they have come up with instruments that are very similar to those that would have been used in the days of David. Micah makes harps such as the one in the picture, and Shoshanna plays them. Jewish tradition says that the Messiah will not come until the harp sounds again in Jerusalem and now, for the first time in many centuries, harps are being made and played in the ancient city.

We have already seen that critics argued that David could not have played on an instrument of ten strings, but archaeological evidence has shown that such instruments were known long before David's time. (Earlier we saw evidences of that from both Ur and Egypt.)

Critics also claimed that David could not have written psalms attributed to him: that they should be dated 800 years later, in the Maccabean period. We shall see that based on findings at Ras Shamra (the ancient Ugarit) in Syria, the famous Professor W.F. Albright endorsed the fact that the psalms of David should be dated to David's own time.

Professor William Foxwell Albright

Professor William Foxwell Albright was one of the world's greatest archaeologists. He came virtually semicircle over the years to a point of recognizing the historical as well as the spiritual integrity of the Christian Scriptures.

Dr. Clifford Wilson took this photograph of the late Professor W.F. Albright outside his apartment near Johns Hopkins University in Baltimore in 1969.

Early in his career Professor Albright had little respect for the historical accuracy of the Old Testament records. This attitude changed as years went by: his own researches convinced him that the Bible records of history should be taken seriously. Before his death he was contributing to such conservative Christian journals as *Christianity Today*.

After some hours of "archaeological discussion" on this occasion, there was the opportunity to discuss personal faith. In response to a question about "faith," Professor Albright stated, "Dr. Wilson, I didn't want to die as so many of my liberal friends will die, believing nothing." He went on to tell of his personal faith commitment to "the Christ of the Gospels."

From that moment the two men were in a different relationship — not just an academic giant (arguably the man who has made the greatest impact ever on biblical archaeology) and a younger scholar, but now known to each other as brethren in Christ.

Looking Down into a Valley from Jerusalem

And it came to pass in an eveningtide, that David arose from off his bed, and walked upon the roof of the king's house: and from the roof he saw a woman washing herself; and the woman was very beautiful to look upon (2 Sam. 11:2).

He sent for her, and soon after that she told him she was pregnant. David was not only guilty of adultery, but of murder also, for he had the woman's husband, Uriah the Hittite, deliberately murdered in

Looking Down on Silwan Village from Upper Jerusalem

This picture illustrates the way David could have looked down and seen Bath-sheba as she bathed. Bath-sheba should have known that she could be seen from above and, although David was guilty, it is probable that Bath-sheba was also guilty.

battle. David eventually was forced to confess his sin, and he knew the judgment of God because of it.

David's sin was grievous. Nevertheless, it is also true that he was possibly provoked. This picture shows the sort of outlook that David would have had (though this is not the exact area, as the original Mount Zion is still unexcavated). The reference in 2 Samuel 11 makes it clear that David was able to see this woman from the rooftop. She also should have known that she could be seen, and should not have exposed herself. Sometimes geographic factors are important to help us to understand incidents that are recorded in Scripture.

Excavations in Israel by Dame Kathleen Kenyon

Dr. Kathleen Kenyon became famous for her excavations both at Jerusalem and Jericho. Some of her conclusions have not stood investigation at both those sites, it being claimed that she made conclusions that were not justified by the relatively small amount of evidence in the limited spaces that she excavated.[26]

Nevertheless, some of her results are very important. One was that she showed that the pool of Siloam was inside the city of Jerusalem in David's time. Earlier critics had claimed that it was outside the walls of the city.

David's men conquered Jerusalem by means of the "tsinor" — the water tunnel, or "gutter" as it is translated in 2 Samuel 5:8. Because it seemed that the pool of Siloam was OUTSIDE the city, Professor W.F. Albright suggested that a similar Canaanite word meaning "hook" was intended — thus implying

Part of the Excavation of Jerusalem

This is part of the excavations of Jerusalem conducted by Dr. Kathleen Kenyon. They were of considerable interest, though there has been criticism that some of her conclusions were based on insufficient evidence, both at Jerusalem and Jericho.

that David's men scaled the wall in order to capture the city. Dr. Kenyon showed that the pool of Siloam was INSIDE the city, and the "tunnel" has again been recognized as the way the city was entered.

We have already seen that there were carefully camouflaged channels from outside Canaanite cities to the water supply inside.

Pool of Siloam

This is the pool of Siloam in Jerusalem as it is today, and dates back to Roman times. Some of the Roman pillars can actually be seen built into the structure — perhaps (but not certainly) reminding us of a time when 18 men were killed when pillars fell on them, as referred to by the Lord Jesus Christ.

We saw that in David's time his men captured the city via the "tsinor" (water tunnel). The critics had claimed

that although this water tunnel led to the pool of Siloam, the walls of Jerusalem were still further up the hill. They argued that even if the men did reach the pool of Siloam, they would not have been able to overpower the guards and capture the city.

Dr. Kathleen Kenyon's excavations showed that the walls of the city of David's time extended further down the hill than earlier archaeologists had believed. The casual comment about the "tsinor" was excellent local color.

Another View of the Pool of Siloam

This boy acted out the story of the blind man whom Jesus sent to the pool of Siloam for healing.
Siloam was of interest both in David's time, and in that of our Lord on earth. A Byzantine
church and later a mosque were built over the pool.

Through the tunnel on the right-hand side there is the exit that leads out to the spring Gihon, a spring that is well outside the city. This was the extension to the Jebusite tunnel that was known earlier, in David's time, but the extension itself was undertaken in the days of King Hezekiah.

In 1880 a boy entered the tunnel from the Siloam end and found the famous Siloam inscription. The prominent archaeologist, Professor A.H. Sayce, made a copy of the inscription, sitting in the mud till late hours of the night. He reported that it told the way the workmen came from opposite ends to build this extended tunnel in the days of King Hezekiah.

The pool of Siloam is also of special interest to Christian students because it was to this pool that the Lord Jesus Christ sent a man born blind. When he washed his eyes as directed by our Lord, the man received his sight. The word "Siloam" means "sent," and as well as this being a physical, literal healing that could only be attributed to the powers of the Lord Jesus Christ, it is also a story with a spiritual meaning. It is only as we come to the One who was "sent" by the Father that we, too, have spiritual sight.

The Traditional Tomb of Absalom

Traditionally, Jewish people regard this tomb on the left as that of Absalom. Others claim that the other two tombs are of one of the James' of the New Testament and of the Old Testament prophet Zechariah. The identification is not certain.

Absalom was David's son who traitorously attempted to take over David's throne.

> Now Absalom in his lifetime had taken and set up a pillar for himself, which is in the King's Valley. For he said, "I have no son to keep my name in remembrance." He called the pillar after his own name. And to this day it is called Absalom's Monument (2 Sam. 18:18).

The building itself is impressive, being 47 feet high, its lower portion being a mass of solid rock that has been detached from the face of the cliff by the passages hewn through it. These are about 9 feet high, and are adorned with "Ionic" columns. Within the upper structure there is a room about 8 feet square.

It is possible that the monument might have been carved out of the stone on the instructions of Absalom, but it is widely agreed that the adornments on the outside of the pillar have been added at a later time. It is usually agreed that the pillar itself dates to about the second or first century B.C.

"So David Slept with His Fathers"

In 1 Kings 2 we read of David's death, preceded by a series of injunctions to Solomon, whom David had pronounced as his successor. Solomon's anointing as king is recorded in I Kings 1.

In chapter 2 David specifically mentioned the death of Absalom, and instructed Solomon to avenge Absalom's death (verses 5 and 6). Even as he approached death David still demonstrated a revengeful side to his nature.

That example was taken up by Solomon himself in another way, for soon after David's death he took an early opportunity to have his older half-brother Adonijah put to death. Adonijah was Absalom's younger brother (1 Kings 1:6).

Adonijah had conspired to take the throne before Solomon himself had been anointed. Solomon's mother was Bath-sheba, and she was involved in out-playing Adonijah so that her own son Solomon took the throne, and then in providing an excuse for Solomon to execute his rival Adonijah (1 Kings 1:5, 11-40, 2:13-25).

This is NOT where David was buried — the actual area of his city is largely unexcavated. These boxes were in a vault at the so-called "Church of Tears" in Jerusalem. They illustrate the Jewish practice of burying bones together in such receptacles.

"King David's Tomb"

In 1 Kings 2:10 we read that King David was buried "in the city of David" — and that was on the eastern hill of Jerusalem. For various reasons, such as the non-accessibility in modern times of the eastern hill at the level of David's reign, the western hill has become known (incorrectly) as Zion. The idea of David's tomb being there goes back about 1,000 years, but it has no actual basis as fact.

Even as late as the time of the Crusaders this site was not taken seriously as the tomb of David. However, in the 15th century A.D. a new attitude developed. Jerome Murphy-O'Connor states:

Both Jews and Muslims remained highly skeptical until the C.15 when the legend

"To King David's Tomb"

This sign is of interest, but only to remind us that the people believed that King David was buried somewhere in Jerusalem. Scholars agree that this is not on the true "Mount Zion."

of treasures buried with the king ("Antiquities," 16:179-182) gripped the imagination; then it became important to get the Franciscans out of the building which they had restored in the early C.14.[27]

The site of the so-called "Tomb of David" has great sentimental value, but it is not accepted as such by scholars today.

So-Called "David's Tomb" in Jerusalem

The Jewish people prayed for the return of David to be their king, and they needed some place that they could revere as his burial-place. In this picture a traditional Jewish worshiper prays in front of the so-called tomb of David. The golden crowns at the site of the tomb are in honor of their great monarch of 3,000 years ago. The Jewish people have added many gold crowns since 1948 when Israel was declared a nation.

We again comment that this is NOT the true tomb of David. At the time this identification was made, the true Mount Zion had not been excavated. Nehemiah 3:16 refers to the sepulchers of David as part of Nehemiah's systematic description of the layout of Jerusalem as the wall was repaired. It is clear that David was buried "between Shiloh and the house of the mighty men" (the guardhouse) on the eastern hill.

This room is in the same building as the Cenacle which is identified as the room where the Last Supper was held. However, the building itself would have been destroyed by the troops of Titus in A.D. 70. The site is thus also suspect as the place where the Last Supper was held.

Sculpture at Gethsemane

This is a carving in stone outside one of the sites identified as the Garden of Gethsemane. It is at least in the general area of the garden where our Lord was in agony.

Old Testament prophets looked on to the sorrow and sufferings of Christ. In one of his Psalms David even wrote, "Even my own familiar friend in whom I trusted, Who ate my bread, Has lifted up his heel against me" (Ps. 41:9). David was prophetically looking on to the time when Judas Iscariot would betray his Lord. Judas did that, betraying his Lord for 30 pieces of silver as foretold in Zechariah 11:12. Then in the Garden of Gethsemane Judas betrayed our Lord with a kiss.

This picture shows the Lord Jesus Christ being arrested in the Garden of Gethsemane, about to be taken off before the Jewish leaders who then demanded that He be executed. They sent Him on to Pontius Pilate after their own false trial. He was arraigned before Pilate, the representative of one of the greatest systems of justice the world had ever known, but was declared innocent. Pilate announced that he found no fault in Him, and when He was sent to Herod, Jesus was again "acquitted." Yet Pilate, who announced a number of times that he found no fault in our Lord, would have signed His execution warrant.

In the Garden of Gethsemane our Lord's agony was like great drops of blood falling to the ground as He cried, "O My Father, if it is possible, let this cup pass from Me; nevertheless, not as I will, but as You will" (Matt. 26:39).

Gethsemane was divine triumph rather than human tragedy. As we have seen, these happenings in Gethsemane were foretold, because that was where the one who was His friend lifted up his hand against Him, having sold his Lord for 30 pieces of silver (Ps. 41:9; Zech. 11:12; Mark 14:10; Matt. 26:15).

The Cross, the Crook, and the Crown

The crucifixion itself was also accurately portrayed by David, 1,000 years before it happened. These are remarkable extracts from David's Psalm 22:

My God, My God, why have You forsaken me? (Ps. 22:1).
(Also quoted by our Lord on the cross.)

All those who see Me ridicule Me (Ps. 22:7).

I am poured out like water, And all My bones are out of joint (Ps. 22:14).

They pierced My hands and My feet (Ps. 22:16).

They divide My garments among them, And for My clothing they cast lots (Ps. 22:18).

I will declare Your name to my brethren; In the midst of the assembly I will praise You (Ps. 22:22).

It is as though David came a thousand years through the centuries, sat at the foot of the cross, and described our Lord's sufferings and subsequent victory as He ascended to the Father's right hand. Psalms 22, 23, and 24 have been called "The Cross, The Crook (of the Shepherd), and the Crown" — pointing to the victories beyond the grave, with Jesus ultimately crowned. How did David know? Scripture itself gives the answer, "Holy men of God spoke as they were moved by the Holy Spirit" (2 Pet. 1:21).

Christ Is Risen . . . and Ascended!

This picture by Lisa Flentge brings together a number of spiritual principles relating to the physical resurrection and the literal ascension of our Lord Jesus Christ. On the left she has pictured an angel outside the empty tomb, reminding us of the earlier angelic announcement, "He is not here — He is risen!" Then we are reminded of Luke who tells us that as our Lord ascended His hands were outstretched in blessing towards the watching disciples. In the right background we see rejoicing heavenly beings as they wait to welcome home the Lord of life — our Saviour.

Section V

A Brief Summary

We have seen that both Saul and David "come to life" in the light of archaeological findings. These touch Saul's fortress at Gibeah, Saul's death on Mt. Gilboah and his body taken to Beth-shean, the site of the contest between young men at the pool of Gibeon, the fact of ten-stringed instruments being known long before David's time, and David's psalms being clearly set against the background of his time. This last has been confirmed by important finds at Ras Shamra, the ancient Ugarit.

The Ras Shamra Tablets

Ras Shamra was first excavated by Claude F.A. Schaeffer in 1929 after a chance discovery by a Syrian plowing his field. The excavations by Schaeffer continued until 1939: they were resumed by others in later years. There were five major occupation levels, but those dating from the 15th and early 14th centuries B.C. were most important as to the information they yielded. There was a large cemetery with magnificent vases and many things relating to commercial art, including a set of weights with Egyptian motifs. There was even a well-preserved bronze figure of the Egyptian god Horus.

Over 600 tablets were found in a new script which seemed to be cuneiform, but eventually it turned out to be an alphabetical writing that had 30 cuneiform signs. It was a previously unknown Semitic language, closely related to Hebrew and other Semitic dialects that were spoken in the land of Canaan.

The tablets were mainly religious texts in poetic form, and they told a great deal about religious beliefs and practices. It therefore became possible for Bible students to understand much more than previously about the religion of the Canaanites against whom the Israelites campaigned under Joshua and his successors.

Most importantly, the findings at Ras Shamra demonstrated the integrity of the psalms of David. As Professor W.F. Albright stated after these findings, "To attribute such Psalms to the Maccabean period is absurd."

Archaeology Endorses Bible Incidents

As we have proceeded through this series of photographs, we have seen that archaeology demonstrates the superiority of Bible records, throws light on customs and local color, clarifies the meanings of words, and shows that the Bible refers correctly to particular peoples, even using their language as appropriate.

It demonstrates that specific incidents have been confirmed, and at times archaeology even adds to our knowledge of some Bible people and incidents. At other times it becomes clear that the Bible writers have given nobler and higher significance to local background and language. We do not claim that archaeology "proves the Bible," for that would wrongly put archaeology above the Bible. However, we do show that archaeology has led to a remarkable re-acceptance of the Bible as a wonderful Book of history — the greatest the world has ever seen.

We are not surprised: the Lord Jesus Christ himself stated, "Your Word is truth" (John 17:17). And He himself is its central theme.

SECTION VI

A GREATER THAN DAVID IS HERE

David — The Man After God's Own Heart

"I have found David the son of Jesse, a man after My own heart, who will do all My will" (Acts 13:22).

In this section we are discussing the life of David, the man after God's own heart.

It is important to notice that if Israel had waited, God would have given them the right man as king, even David the son of Jesse. But in their impatience they went against God and wanted "a king to judge us like all the nations" — and in so doing they were rejecting God, as the Lord himself told Samuel (1 Sam. 8:57). Humanly speaking, Saul was physically ideal. Spiritually he left much to be desired.

Pointers to Kingship in Israel

Even before Saul's anointing there were pointers to the need for a king in Israel. This was to be God's way to consolidate the nation and to preserve her independence in times of tremendous stress. There were external foes such as the Philistines, and because of the constant likelihood of attack it was most desirable that all the tribes of Israel be united.

There were problems associated with that nationhood, including the feeling among some tribes that they were geographically isolated. There are real indications that at times tribal jealousies of various types prevented the effective welding together of the tribes into a united whole, and tribal clashes are recorded in Joshua 22 and in Judges 12, 19, and 20.

Throughout the Book of Judges we are reminded that these people were not really united in their desire for a single leader. But there are occasional pointers to kingship, such as when Gideon delivered his people (Judg. 8:22-23) but refused the kingship, and also when Gideon's son Abimelech tried to make himself king (Judg. 9:6).

There also were factors which united Israel, and these included their common language and origin, their national adherence to the law of Moses, and the worship of Jehovah based on their unique covenant relationship with Him.

When it was seen that the sons of Samuel did not walk in his ways the people began to ask for "a king to lead us, such as all the other nations have" (1 Sam. 8:5;NIV). Archaeology throws considerable light on the sort of oppression towards which the Israelites were heading. If they were to have a king like all the other nations, this would mean military conscription, the confiscation of their personal lands, the introduction of heavy taxation, and forced labor. This is the picture we see from Canaanite documents found at two ancient sites, at Alalakh and at Ras Shamra.

Nevertheless, the people were determined, and so they accepted Saul, who was a man of great physical attraction, but who was not a "man after God's own heart." Saul started well, for he was a young man of outstanding promise, but he soon gave quite unacceptable evidence of becoming the type of king they wanted. When he presumed by taking to himself priestly offices which were forbidden to him, he showed grave failure as to spiritual principles. He began to put himself above Jehovah, and this was not acceptable as a pattern of kingship in Israel.

God Himself Was Israel's King

It has been rightly said that Israel was never meant to be other than a theocracy — God himself was their King. The human king was but the "vice gerent (vice regent) for Jehovah," the one who would act as His representative.

Digressing for a moment, it is interesting to note how God allowed His prophets to challenge the king when the king acted in a way that was offensive to Jehovah. Thus, Samuel rebuked Saul when Saul took to himself those priestly functions; Nathan brought the Lord's message of rebuke when David was responsible for the death of Uriah the Hittite; Elijah came suddenly into the presence of King Ahab to tell him the very elements would oppose him, for Ahab had introduced the worship of Baal who was supposed to control those elements. Baal was shown to be utterly powerless against the true God, Jehovah.

Let us return to the days of Saul, and we find that God rejected Saul because of Saul's own folly. Toward the end of his life, this man with such outstanding promise had to declare, "I have played the fool" (1 Sam. 26:21). Saul, the son of Kish, had indeed played the fool, and God had rejected him from the kingship. However, God always has His man, and He had sent the prophet Samuel to Bethlehem, later to be the birthplace of our Lord. There young David, the shepherd boy, was anointed as the future king of Israel.

David formed a wonderful friendship with Jonathan, the son of Saul, and that friendship has become known throughout the world and down through the centuries as one of the most beautiful ever recorded between men. This is the background to the beautiful lament which came so clearly from the very heart of David as he sorrowed when Saul and Jonathan died on Mt. Gilboa in a battle against the Philistines (2 Sam. 1:17).

This was the end of an era. Saul had been the people's choice, one who towered above them in stature. Yet this giant of a man had not ventured against the Philistine champion, though he had been prepared to allow the stripling David to go against him. Throughout the story of David we see many ways in which this young man was indeed a man after God's own heart.

We also recognize something of his failure, demonstrating to us the wonderful grace of God. Thus, we who also fail at times can take courage: God knows the desire of our hearts to serve Him, and He is ever ready to cleanse us and to empower us afresh for His service.

David Anointed as King

As we study the life of David we find there are some spiritual reminders of the fact that a greater-than-David Is here." Thus, we read in Psalm 23:5:

> You prepare a table before me in the presence of my enemies; You anoint my head with oil; my cup runs over.

This verse from that famous psalm of David has been learned by many thousands through the centuries. We shall briefly see some of the ways in which the truths of this verse were fulfilled in the personal life of David himself.

In his younger days he was a faithful shepherd, quietly looking after the interests of his family, but the day came when he was anointed for a more important work. The prophet Samuel appeared one day in Bethlehem, and he came to the house of Jesse, David's father, for the Lord had told Samuel that one of Jesse's sons was to be the new king.

Saul had proved a failure in God's eyes, and now God had found a man after His own heart (1 Sam. 13:14). Samuel located him in the town where David's greater Son ????? was to be born about a thousand years later.

The older sons of Jesse were first presented before Samuel, and each time as these several sons came forward Samuel thought, *This is the right man!* But when the last of the older brothers had come, Samuel still had no word from the Lord to anoint any one of them.

When he asked if there was not another, he was told there was only David, the lad out with the sheep. David was called, and he was the one chosen of the Lord. He was considered so insignificant that even his father Jesse had not thought of him as the Lord's chosen. His brothers obviously had no thought as to David's special election.

In this we have a faint picture of our Lord, for we read that even His brethren did not believe in Him (John 7:5). At an early age our Lord knew of His anointing, for in Luke 2:49 He reminded Mary and Joseph that He must be about His Father's business (His Father's house). In that scene at the temple where our Lord showed himself to be someone so much after God's own heart, we see a similarity to David, the lad who also was after God's own heart and was anointed by Samuel in front of his brothers. It is written of our Lord himself, "I will declare Your name to My brethren; In the midst of the assembly I will praise You" (Ps. 22:22).

The day came when David was sent by his father to visit his brothers on the battlefield, bringing them necessary provisions. When he arrived a giant was challenging the chosen people and mocking them because they were not prepared to send a champion to fight him. The story is well-known, and it was not long before David had slain the boasting giant, Goliath. However, before David was allowed to venture against this opponent he was tested in various ways. His brothers thought he was simply an upstart, and even before he was brought before King Saul his qualifications were seriously challenged.

Though very young, David had already proved himself, especially when he defended his sheep against wild animals. No doubt his claims could have been substantiated by others there, probably including his own brothers. Otherwise it seems unlikely he would have been allowed to venture against Goliath.

Saul at first wanted David to wear the king's own heavy armor, but David recognized that his strength was of the Lord. So he went against the giant, relying only in the quiet assurance that the Lord was with him. The giant himself mocked at David, saying such things as, "Am I a dog, that you come to me with sticks?" (1 Sam. 17:43). But David knew better, and he told the boasting giant that he came in the name of the Lord of hosts. And that was sufficient. With but one of his stones carefully chosen from the brook, David killed Goliath and then ran and cut off his head. For the moment the threat to Israel was ended.

A Greater-Than-Goliath Is Defeated

Our Lord Jesus Christ came to His own brethren, the Jewish people, and they challenged His rights and his qualifications in regard to His activities associated with a battle greater than that fought by David, for Jesus was engaged in the great battle for the soul. They did not understand the power that was His, and they had no confidence in His ability.

The Lord Jesus Christ has come against another giant — not just a Goliath — but against the prince of the power of the air, Satan. He would, if possible, deceive the very elect. Jehovah heard the taunting of this one, and "when the fullness of the time had come, God sent forth His Son, born of a woman, born under the law, to redeem those who were under the law" (Gal. 4:4-5).

Christ met HIS Goliath and defeated him on Mount Calvary. The seed of the woman had crushed the serpent's head (Gen. 3:15). The forces of evil were scattered. The victory is eternal.

Anointed — But Enthronement Delayed

Various incidents followed in the life of David, but our purpose is to see similarities to the life of our Lord. It became known to many in Israel that David was to be their new king, but though he had been anointed, David had to wait some years before he was enthroned. The very fact of David's popularity led to hatred on the part of Saul.

In passing, we mention that Saul is one of the greatest enigmas in Scripture. He started off so well and had such potential, and yet pride and self-will led to his downfall. This handsome young man followed a sad downward trail until ultimately we see him in touch with those who were supposedly in contact with the dead, in the incident with the witch of Endor.

Before David knew what it was to be accepted as king he first knew what it was to be a fugitive, and the famous incident at the Cave of Adullam took place:

> David therefore departed from there and escaped to the cave of Adullam. And when his brothers and all his father's house heard it, they went down there to him. And everyone who was in distress, everyone who was in debt, and everyone who was discontented gathered to him. So he became captain over them. And there were about four hundred men with him (1 Sam. 22:1-2).

This unlikely band was to be the nucleus of David's faithful allies. Their numbers grew until ultimately he was accepted as king, first over Judah and then over all the tribes of Israel.

How like our Lord all this is! He knew what it was to be rejected before He was exalted, and to have an unlikely band seek Him out when the great ones of the world ridiculed His claims. He still says, "Come to Me, all you who labor and are heavy laden, and I will give you rest" (Matt. 11:28). Those in distress came to David and they found purpose and satisfaction, and so it is in a far more wonderful way with the Lord Jesus Christ. Everyone in debt came to David. All who come to the Lord Jesus Christ are in spiritual debt, for the wages of sin is death (Rom. 6:23). He took the penalty on himself and paid the debt of those who come to Him. The world rejected Him at Calvary, but His friends own Him and go to Him outside the camp, bearing His reproach (Heb. 13:13). As the well-known hymn says:

> Our Lord is now rejected, and by the world disowned,
> By the many still neglected, but by the few enthroned.

Those who were discontented came to David, and in life today many people are discontented and do not know why. The reason is that man is body, soul, and spirit, and cannot find full satisfaction until he knows the joy of spiritual fellowship with God. Then, and only then, can he live to the fullest capacity of body, soul, and spirit. It is not enough to have physical satisfaction, nor to know the enjoyment of the soul and of the mind, but one must have spiritual fellowship with God before he can know continual peace and satisfaction. We are made in the image of God and, like David, we need to be men after God's own heart. Then, like the early disciples of the Lord Jesus Christ, we will hear Him say, "My peace I give to you."

David at times gave a very wonderful demonstration of love for his enemies — a concept that many in Israel simply did not know. Even in the days of the Dead Sea Scroll community, Jewish leaders were writing about hating their enemies, declaring that they should be slain mercilessly. King Saul became

David's enemy, and on at least two occasions David could have taken the king's life, but he would not do so. He showed true nobility of spirit and godliness as he refused to stretch forth his hand against the Lord's anointed.

We see the perfection of this teaching in the life of the Lord Jesus Christ who said, "Love your enemies, bless those who curse you, do good to those who hate you, and pray for those who spitefully use you and persecute you" (Matt. 5:44). He showed this to perfection in His own life, and even in death as He cried, "Father, forgive them, for they do not know what they do" (Luke 23:34).

Though David was for some time rejected by his people, in that time of rejection we saw also that many dissatisfied people gathered to him at the Cave of Adullam. Eventually they were to know the joy of seeing David crowned as king, first in Hebron over Judah, and then in Jerusalem over Judah and Israel combined.

We who have gone forth to Christ outside the camp, bearing His reproach, will one day see Him acknowledged as King of kings and Lord of lords: "At the name of Jesus every knee should bow, of those in heaven, and of those on earth, and of those under the earth, and that every tongue should confess that Jesus Christ is Lord, to the glory of God the Father" (Phil. 2:10-11).

When David was eventually made king of the combined nation, he made Jerusalem its capital. All power is given to our Lord in heaven and in earth, and when we go to the end of Revelation we find that the New Jerusalem comes down out of heaven and becomes the dwelling place of God among men. The Jerusalem of David's day was very special, and the city became recognized as the place where God's name was caused to dwell. How much more is this true of the New Jerusalem where God dwells with His people eternally!

Absalom ... and Mephibosheth

Another interesting parallel with our Lord is that of David's relations with his own son, Absalom. Perhaps no more pathetic poem has ever been recorded in literature than David's lament over Absalom, "O my son Absalom — my son, my son Absalom — if only I had died in your place! O Absalom my son, my son!" (2 Sam. 18:33). Absalom was a handsome young man, and the description of his stature and cunning is given in 2 Samuel, commencing at chapter 13. He opposed David and for a time usurped his father's throne. David had to flee, but though Absalom thought he had successfully gained the crown, his triumph was short-lived and soon David was restored to the throne.

The description of Absalom in 2 Samuel 14:25 reminds us at times of the things said about the devil himself. He is transformed into an angel of light (2 Cor. 11:14), and some believe that the description of Lucifer, the son of the morning, actually applies to Satan (Isa. 14:12). He is cunning, as we are reminded in the story of the Garden of Eden. He is ready to distort the words of God, in the temptations of Christ.

In this we are reminded of the way Absalom twisted the affairs of the kingdom so that he himself gained the favor of the people. He set out to gain false popularity and usurp the rights of another (2 Samuel 15). Satan is always prepared to offer popularity and false gains so that he can usurp the rights of Jesus Christ in a man's life, but his victory is short-lived, for the accomplishments of Calvary are eternal.

Seated with the King

The story of Mephibosheth is told in 2 Samuel 9, and in his association with David we again see some interesting parallels to the life of the Lord Jesus Christ. Mephibosheth was dropped by his nurse when he was a child. As a result he was lame from early childhood. Mephibosheth was taken to live at a place called Lodebah, which can be interpreted "No Pasture," or "Nothing." There he was in a place of dissatisfaction and want.

One day messengers from David came, and he was brought into the presence of the king. David had asked the question, "Is there still anyone left of the house of Saul, that I may show him kindness for Jonathan's sake?" (2 Sam. 9:1). It was not for Mephibosheth's own sake but for Jonathan's sake that Mephibosheth was sent for, and brought into the presence of the king. His property was restored, and he was given the privilege of sitting in the presence of the king, his lameness now covered.

In this we have a lovely illustration of the Lord Jesus Christ. God has loved us, not for our own sakes, but for Jesus' sake. We are reminded of this faintly as we see David seeking Mephibosheth, not for his sake but for Jonathan's sake.

We, too, have been in a place of "no pasture," of no spiritual enjoyment, in desperate need, but the King has sent for us! He invites us to His banqueting house, and His banner over us is love. We need not fear, as no doubt Mephibosheth did at first, for the King's desire is always towards us and He wants us to eat at His table.

We are reminded in Ephesians 2:6 that we are seated with Christ in the heavenlies. Not only is our lameness covered at the table of the King, but the Lord has restored our strength, so that we walk and leap and praise God. We are like that man who was healed of his lameness, recorded in Acts 3:8. He did not hide his lameness, for it was gone. He became an active follower of Jesus.

Also, we have spiritual restoration — we are made spiritually whole by Him who has become our King, even David's greater Son. It is indeed true that a greater-than-David is here.

A Greater-Than-David Is Here

If David then calls Him "Lord," how is He his Son?" (Matt. 22:45).

Our quotation comes at the end of a series of questions our Lord asked of the Pharisees who had tried to entangle Him in His talk. They had combined with their opponents of the Herodian party because of their joint opposition to the Lord Jesus Christ who claimed to be the Messiah, the Son of God. Then the Sadducees had attempted to ridicule our Lord, and a lawyer also had ventured into the fray.

It is remarkable that these three groups would combine as they did at this time. The Pharisees were legalistic literalists, and many of them went to extremes in their interpretation of the meaning of the Law. Even the spirit of the Law was bypassed so long as a literal and formal obedience could be demonstrated. Jesus referred to them as "hypocrites," and of course His description was very appropriate. He described them as whited tombs, clean in outward appearance but actually the inside was full of the bones of the dead.

One example of their ability to manipulate the teaching of the Law is in the well-known argument about how far a man could travel on a Sabbath day. Having traveled a Sabbath day's journey he then must stop, but what was to prevent him now making another Sabbath day's journey? Thus, by a series of brief halts a man could overcome the problem, and travel as far as he liked. By this interpretation he was technically within the law, but, of course, he was utterly opposed to the true spiritual meaning of the Sabbath being a day of rest.

The Sadducees on the other hand were the rationalists of the day. They tended to believe only those things which could be demonstrated by visible evidence. They did not believe in angels or the resurrection from the dead. They did not accept the authority of the Old Testament prophets and writings, but limited themselves to the law of Moses (the first five books of the Bible).

In this connection it is enlightening to see the way in which our Lord answered their question which touched on the resurrection, for He referred to the Law, which they accepted as authoritative, and pointed out that the Law itself spoke of the God of Abraham, of Isaac, and of Jacob. As our Lord said, "God is not the God of the dead, but of the living" (Matt. 22:32). This, of course, implied that Abraham, Isaac, and Jacob lived beyond the grave. Thus, the Sadducees were silenced by the very Law which they accepted.

The Herodian party was quite happy to accept the rule and authority of the several Herods (Herod the Great, followed by his sons), and because of this they were despised by the orthodox Jews who regarded the Idumaean family of Herod as ineligible to assume any form of authority over the Jews. The Idumaeans were the descendants of Esau, and there was very real rivalry between them and orthodox Jews.

Summarizing then, the Sadducees and the Pharisees were poles apart in their religious thinking, and in turn they were as far removed politically from the Herodian party. Yet these three very opposite points of the triangle came together in an attempt to ridicule the teachings of Christ.

We find that instead of our Lord being entangled in His talk, His opponents were confused. Matthew tells us that they marveled, and from that time no one dared ask Him such questions again.

At the end of the "debate" our Lord himself had a question to ask:

> While the Pharisees were gathered together, Jesus asked them, saying, "What do you think about the Christ? Whose Son is He?" They said to Him, "The Son of David." He said to them, "How then does David in the Spirit call him 'Lord,' saying: 'The Lord said to my Lord, "Sit at My right hand, Till I make your enemies your footstool" '? "If David then calls Him 'Lord,' how is He his Son?" And no one was able to answer Him a word, nor from that day on did anyone dare question Him any more (Matt. 22:41-46).

The question Christ asked was a logical one. The Jews themselves recognized their fathers as worthy of honor and respect, and yet our Lord was able to quote from their own authoritative Scriptures to show that the mighty King David had addressed as Lord, One who would be his own descendant.

The genealogy of our Lord Jesus Christ demonstrates that He is the Son of David, and the Jews could not and would not have challenged Him on this point. At that time Jewish family trees were well-authenticated, and if our Lord's claims had not been genuine they would have been easily refuted during His earthly ministry. However, His genealogy was never challenged, because He was who He claimed to be — the Son of David. He was indeed David's greater Son. By implication in this dialogue, Jesus was showing the Jews that their reasoning was incomplete, and that their expected Messiah must indeed be a man, the Son of David, and yet more than a man, the very Son of God. In His own person he claimed to combine these two truths.

Implicit in our Lord's statement was His quiet insistence as to His own superiority to David, for David looked through the centuries and called his own Son, "Lord."

David and Our Lord: A Comparison and a Contrast

It is spiritually profitable for us to compare the lives of David and our Lord and to see some of the ways in which our Lord's superiority is clearly demonstrated.

David was born in Bethlehem, which literally means "House of Bread." Four hundred years later, the prophet Micah was to prophesy concerning that same little town of Bethlehem and to declare that this would be the birthplace of Him whose going forth had been from everlasting, of Him who would be the ruler over Israel. Interestingly enough, Micah prophesied regarding the correct Bethlehem, for there is more than one. He specified that it would be Bethlehem-Ephratah, Ephratah (meaning "fruitful") being an ancient name for this part of Judah.

There is a story of an American journalist who was sent to Bethlehem to report the activities there on Christmas Day. He arrived in Bethlehem on the eve of Christmas Day only to find that he was in the wrong Bethlehem — he was many miles to the north of his appointed destination, and had to make a speedy journey to the south.

Micah did not make such a mistake, for he specified that it would be Bethlehem of Judah. God made no mistake when His Holy Spirit inspired Micah, for Bethlehem of Judah to the south was the ancestral home of the line of David, and when the enrolling took place in the days of Herod the Great, Mary and Joseph had to return to that village of Bethlehem. They reached there just in time, for shortly after their arrival the Baby Jesus was born.

We said that Bethlehem means "House of Bread." When our Lord was born in a stable, little did the innkeeper and others in the village realize that the bread of God had been sent down from heaven into their midst. That little Baby was the living bread of God.

David grew up quietly, with little fuss, pushed more or less into the background, for he had so many brothers older than himself. It is interesting to recognize that our Lord also grew up in quietness, and yet in obedience to those chosen of God to care for Him in His boyhood. He was subject to Joseph and Mary.

In his early life David was a shepherd, and a very faithful shepherd at that. When he was challenged as to his capacity to go against the giant Goliath, he replied that he had personally slain both a lion and a bear when these had come against his sheep. He risked his life for the sheep, being faithful in his appointed task. As we remind ourselves so often in this series, our Lord was also faithful, not only in the risking of His life, but in death itself.

However, there is a difference in risking one's life and deliberately giving one's life. The Lord Jesus Christ set His face as a flint to go to Jerusalem, and He told His disciples that the Son of Man would be mocked, spitefully entreated, scourged, spat on, and crucified (Luke 18:32). He said of himself that He was the Good Shepherd who gave His life for the sheep. He came to die.

The Good Shepherd Who Would Give His Life

As we think of David as a shepherd we are reminded of that wonderful psalm, one of many attributed to him — Psalm 23. In that beautiful poem David talks of green pastures beneath his feet, of still waters beside which he is led, of goodness and mercy that follow him, of a table set in front of him, and he looks on beyond this life to his dwelling in the house of the Lord forever.

This has been rightly known as the Shepherd Psalm and that as is sometimes pointed out, Psalms 22, 23, and 24 form a trilogy. Psalm 22 predictively tells of our Lord's death, as He cried "My God, why have You forsaken Me?" Psalm 23 speaks of the Good Shepherd, and Psalm 24 pictures our Lord in Resurrection.

These three have also been referred to as "The Cross, the Crook, and the Crown." It is interesting to compare Psalm 23, which tells of the Shepherd's crook, with our Lord's statement in John 10. There He says that the sheep hear the Shepherd's voice: He calls them by name and He leads them out. When He puts them forth He goes before them, and the sheep follow because they know His voice. They will not follow a stranger, but will flee from him.

David said in Psalm 23, "The Lord is my Shepherd": for he was but a man, and he trusted another to protect and guide him. In John 10:11 the Lord Jesus says, "I am the good shepherd. The good shepherd gives His life for the sheep." In verse 14 He says, "I am the good shepherd; and I know My sheep, and am known by My own." His sheep are safe in His keeping. Truly, a greater-than-David is here.

"How Is He His Son?"

As we conclude, let us again consider our Lord's own question, "If David then calls Him 'Lord,' how is He his Son?" (Matt. 22:45). The chief priest and the Jewish leaders would not recognize that their Messiah from heaven would be both God and man, yet their own Old Testament prophets openly announced the coming of such a One. In Isaiah 9:6-7 we read of a Child to be born, One who would have the government upon His shoulder, and among other titles He is called the mighty God, the Everlasting Father, and the Prince of Peace. In that same passage Isaiah even declared that there would be no end to His government "upon the throne of David" (verse 7).

So when David called his own son, "Lord," He was looking on to the same One of whom Isaiah prophesied. No wonder the Jews could not answer Jesus' question! It is indeed true that a greater-than-David is here.

Endnotes

[1]E.A. Wallis Budge, *The Book of the Dead* (New York, NY: Bell Publishing, 1960), p. 66.

[2]Manfred Lurker, *The Gods and Symbols of Ancient Egypt* (London: Thames & Hudson, 1980), p.11.

[3]Budge, *The Book of the Dead*, p. 108-110.

[4]Ibid., p. 115.

[5]Kenneth Kitchen, *The Illustrated Bible Dictionary* (Wheaton, IL: Intervarsity Fellowship, Tyndale House, 1980), p. 429.

[6]Jack Finegan, *Light from the Ancient East* (Princeton, NJ: Princeton University Press, 1959).

[7]J.H. Breasted, *A History of Egypt* (New York, NY: Scribner's, 1912).

[8]Stephen Quirke and Jeffrey Spencer, eds., *The British Museum Book of Ancient Egypt* (London: British Museum Press, 1992), p. 173.

[9]George Mendenhall, *The Biblical Archaeologist*, vol. 17 (1954), p. 26-46; 50-76; later reprinted as *Law and Covenant in Israel and the Ancient Near East* (Pittsburgh, PA: Biblical Colloquiums, 1955).

[10]Kenneth Kitchen, *Ancient Orient and Old Testament*, (Chicago, IL: Inter-Varsity Press, 1966), p. 98.

[11]Ibid., p. 128.

[12]Ibid., p. 129.

[13]Howard Vos, *Archaeology in Bible Lands* (Chicago, IL: Moody Press, 1977).

[14]Meir Ben-Dov, *In the Shadow of the Temple* (New York, NY: Harper & Row, 1982), p. 34.

[15]John J. Bimson, *Redating the Exodus and Conquest* (Sheffield, England: The Almond Press, 1981).

[16]Meir Ben-Dov, *In the Shadow of the Temple*, p. 34.

[17]Jerome Murphy-O'Connor, *The Holy Land: An Archaeological Guide from Earliest Times to 1700* (New York, NY: Oxford University Press, 1986).

[18]Merrill F. Unger, *Archaeology and the Old Testament* (Grand Rapids, MI: Zondervan, 1954).

[19]Bimson, *Redating the Exodus and Conquest.*

[20]Murphy-O'Connor, *The Holy Land: An Archaeological Guide from Earliest Times to 1700.*

[21]Edward E. Hindsen, *The Philistines in the Old Testament* (Grand Rapids, MI: Baker Book House, 1981).

[22]Ibid.

[23]Ibid.

[24]Ibid.

[25]W.F. Albright, *History, Archaeology and Christian Humanism* (New, York, NY: McGraw Hill, 1964).

[26]Meir Ben-Dov, *In The Shadow Of The Temple*, p. 34.

[27]Murphy-O'Connor, *The Holy Land: An Archaeological Guide from Earliest Times to 1700.*

Selective Bibliography

This bibliography is not complete. Much that is within the volumes of *The Bible Comes Alive* results from a lifetime of personal research and investigation, often on the actual sites where no written records were available.

Albright, William Foxwell. *Yahweh and the Gods of Canaan*. London: University of London, The Athlone Press, 1968.

_____. *The Biblical Period from Abraham to Ezra*. New York, NY: Harper & Row Torch Books, 1963.

Aldred, Cyril. *Egypt to the End of the Old Kingdom*. London: Thames & Hudson, 1982.

Ankerberg, John, John Weldon, and Walter C. Kaiser Jr. *The Case for Jesus the Messiah*. Chattanooga, TN: The John Ankerberg Evang. Assoc., 1989.

Beasley, Walter J. *The Amazing Story of Sodom*. Bombay: Gospel Literature Service, 1957.

Ben-dov, Meir. *In the Shadow of the Temple*. New York, NY: Harper & Row, 1982.

Bimson, John J. *Redating the Exodus and Conquest*. Sheffield, England: The Almond Press, 1981.

Bowden, Michael. *Ape-Man — Fact or Fallacy*. Bromley, England: Sovereign Publications, 1977.

Boyd, Robert T. *A Pictoral Guide to Biblical Archaeology*. Eugene OR: Harvest House Pub., 1981.

Breasted, J.H. *A History of Egypt*. New York, NY: Scribner's, 1912.

_____. *A Brief History of Ancient Times*. London, England: Ginn and Coy., 1967.

Bruce, Francis F. *Israel and the Nations*. Exeter, England: Paternoster Press, 1963.

Budge, E.A. Wallis. *The Book of the Dead*. New York, NY: Bell Publishing Co., 1949.

Campbell, Edward F. and David N. Freedman (eds.). *The Biblical Archaeologist Reader No. 3*. Garden City, NY: Anchor Books, Doubleday, 1970.

Clack, Clem. *The Bible in Focus*. Blackburn South, Victoria, Australia: Donors Inc., 1980.

Davis, John J. and John C. Whitcomb. *A History Of Israel*. Grand Rapids, MI: Baker Book House, 1980.

Finegan, Jack. *Light From The Ancient Past*. Princeton, NJ: Princeton University Press, 1959.

Gish, Duane T. *Evolution: The Challenge of the Fossil Record*. San Diego, CA: Creation Life Publ., 1985.

Goff, Mike R.O. *Fodor's 90 Israel*. New York, NY: Fodor's-Random House, 1989.

Harrison, R.K. *Introduction to the Old Testament*. Grand Rapids, MI: W.B. Eerdmans, 1975.

_____. *Old Testament Times*. Grand Rapids, MI: W.B. Eerdmans, 1970.

Harvey, Jeff and Charles Pallagy. *The Bible and Science*. Blackburn, Victoria, Australia: Acacia Press, 1985.

Hindsen, Edward. *The Philistines and the Old Testament*. Grand Rapids, MI: Baker Book House, 1981.

Josephus, Flavius. *Antiquities of the Jews*. Loeb Classical Lib., Transl. H. St.-J. Thackeray and R. Marcus.

Kitchen, Kenneth A. *Ancient Orient and Old Testament*. Chicago, IL: Inter-Varsity Press, 1966.

_____. *The Bible in Its World*. Downers Grove, IL: Inter-Varsity Press, 1978.

Kramer, Samuel N. "The Babel of Tongues — A Sumerian Version." March 1968. *Journal American Oriental Society*.

Lehman, Manfred R. "Abraham's Purchase of Machpelah and Hittite Law." Bulletin of the American Schools of Oriental Research, No.129, February 1953.

Matthiae, Paolo. Ebla — *An Empire Rediscovered.* Garden City, NY: Doubleday, 1981.

Mendenhall, George E. *Law and Covenant in Israel and the Ancient Near East.* Pittsburgh, PA: The Biblical Colloquium, 1955.

Morris, Henry M. *The Genesis Record.* San Diego, CA: Creation Life Publishers, 1976.

_____. *Evolution in Turmoil.* San Diego, CA: Creation Life Publishers, 1982.

_____. *The Biblical Basis for Modern Science.* Grand Rapids, MI: Baker Book House, 1990.

Morris, Henry M. and Gary E. Parker. *What Is Creation Science?* Green Forest,

AR: Master Books, 1982.

Murphy-O'Connor, Jerome. *An Archaeological Guide of the Holy Land.* New York, NY: Oxford University Press, 1986.

Oxnard, Charles. Nature. (258:389, 1975).

Pfeiffer, Charles, F., ed. *The Biblical World: A Dictionary of Biblical Archaeology.* Grand Rapids, MI: Baker Book House, 1966.

_____. *Ras Shamra and the Bible.* Grand Rapids, MI: Baker Book House, 1963.

_____. *Tell El Amara and the Bible.* Grand Rapids, MI: Baker Book House, 1963.

Pritchard, John B., ed. *Ancient Near Eastern Texts Relating to the New Testament.* Princeton, NJ: Princeton University Press, 1950.

_____. *The Ancient Near East In Pictures Relating to the Old Testament.* Princeton, NJ: Princeton University Press, 1954.

Rendle-Short, John. *Man: Ape or Image.* Sunnybank, Queensland, Australia: Creation Science Publishing, 1981.

Shea, William. "Archaeology and Biblical Research." (Article supplied personally to Dr Bryant Wood and Dr Clifford Wilson.)

Unger, Merrill F. *Archaeology and the Old Testament.* Grand Rapids, MI: Zondervan, 1954.

Vos, Howard F. *Archaeology in Bible Lands.* Chicago, IL: Moody Press, 1977.

Whitcomb, John and Henry Morris. *The Genesis Flood.* Grand Rapids, MI: Baker Book House, 1989.

Whitelaw, Robert L. *Evolution and the Bible in the Light of 15,000 Radio Carbon Dates.* Sterling, VA: Grace Abounding Ministries, 1986.

Wilder-Smith, A.E. *The Natural Sciences Know Nothing of Evolution.* Green Forest, AR: Master Books, 1982.

Wilson, Clifford A. *That Incredible Book the Bible.* Melbourne, Australia: Word of Truth Productions, 1973.

_____. *Rocks, Relics, and Biblical Reliability.* Grand Rapids, MI: Zondervan, 1977.

_____. *Highlights of Biblical Archaeology.* Melbourne, Australia: Pacific College of Graduate Studies, 1985.

_____. *Creation or Evolution : Facts or Fairytales?* Melbourne, Australia: Pacific College of Graduate Studies, 1991.

Wiseman, P.J. *Clues to Creation and Genesis* (edited by Professor Donald J. Wiseman). London: Marshall Morgan and Scott, 1977.

Wiseman, Donald. *Illustrations from Biblical Archaeology*. London: Tyndale Press, 1958.

Wood, Leon J. *A Survey of Israel's History,* revised by David O'Brien, Grand Rapids, MI: Zondervan, 1986.

Woolley, C. Leonard. *Ur of the Chaldees*. London: Penguin Books, 1954.

Wright, G. Ernest. "Philistine Coffins and Mercenaries." *The Biblical Archaeologist*, Vol. 22 1959, p. 54-66.

_____. *Biblical Archaeology*. Philadelphia, PA: Westminster Press, 1962.

Zilnay, *Zev. Israel Guide*. Jerusalem, Ahiever, 56 Jaffa Road, 1969.

Dr. Clifford Wilson is the founding president of

PACIFIC INTERNATIONAL UNIVERSITY

Professional training by academic education including extension studies

Majoring in:

Bible and Theology	Christian Philosophy
Biblical Archaeology	Church Ministry
Christian Counseling	Comparative Religions
Christian Education	Linguistics
Christian Evidences	Trans-cultural studies and Missiology

You don't have to leave home to receive thorough training in Bible, Christian skills, and ministry.

Courses are available at:
Certificate level
Diplomas
Bachelor Degrees
Master Degrees
Doctoral Degrees

Write for our abbreviated catalog:

P.O. Box 1717 (2158 N. Ramsey Ave.), Springfield, MO 65801
(417) 831-7515, Fax: (417) 831-7673
E-mail: wilson@pacificuniversity.com
Web-site: www.pacificuniversity.com